The
BIBLE COLORING BOOK
VOLUME ONE

PRODUCED BY
CHRISTANDKIDS.COM
WONDERVISTA.COM

FEATURING
THE KING JAMES BIBLE
OLD & NEW TESTEMENT
STORIES

This coloring book is illustrated for kids and adults. We hope you have as much fun finishing the artwork, as we did starting it. This is our first Bible themed book. We've added the verses that inspired the art on the back of each page, just in case you'd like to share your work with someone special.

We approached these drawings as artists and readers of the Bible. We did our best to be inspired by what was written in the Bible and not what movies, artists or theologians have added to it over the years. We tried to have fun with the art and we hope you enjoy that!

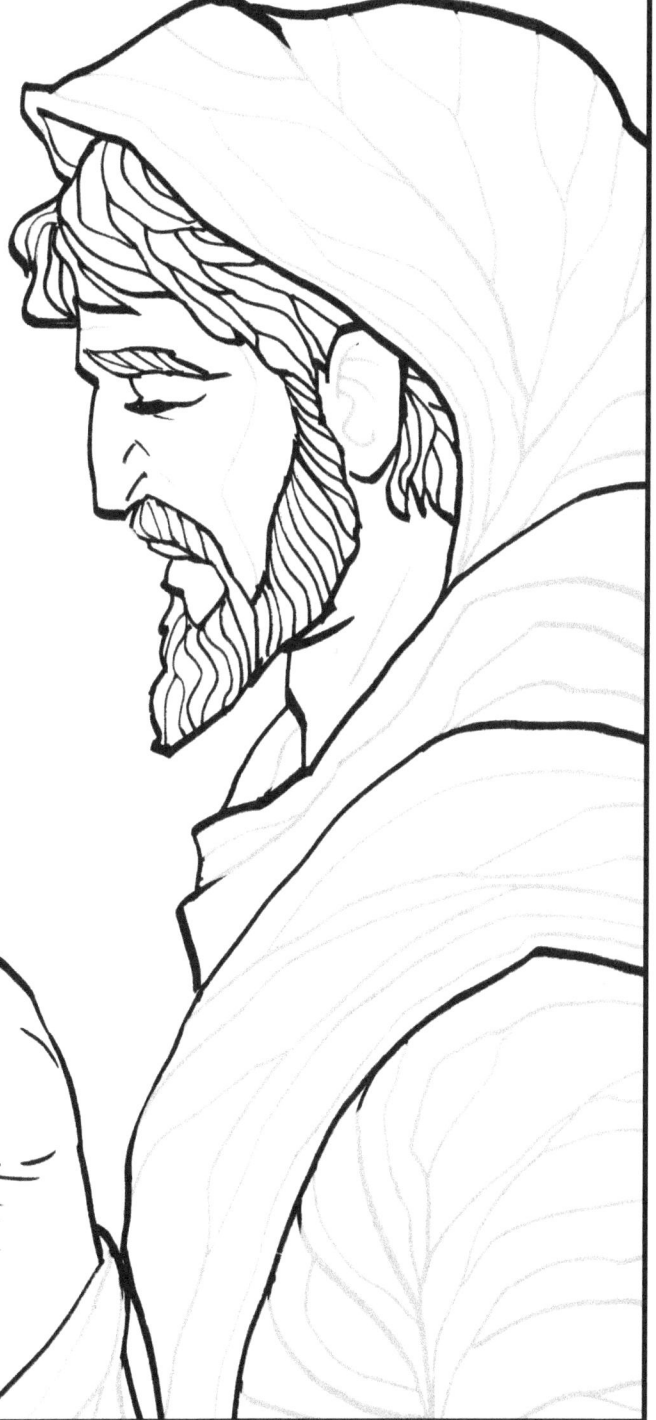

Hi, my name is Will Hughes and I really appreciate your support of this book. If you like it, I will certainly do more... actually, I had so much fun doing this one, I promise I'll do more just so I can have them!

I remember a time when comic books and movies were filled with heroes you could admire and adventures that were safe to enjoy. That's the kind of work I am now dedicating my life to.

So, I wanted to also let you know about the other projects I'm working on. Our website: **www.christandkids.com** along with our original site: **www.jesusandkidz. com** has more downloadable coloring pages and many free illustrated bible stories for you to view and share.

I also produce fun, family friendly, imaginative and sometimes very silly films, comic books and even novels on our primary entertainment site: **www.wondervista.com**

These sites are financially supported by advertisers, product sales and you.

Thanks again for *your* support. It really means so much to me! With your help, I will be able to produce many more enjoyable products, for you.

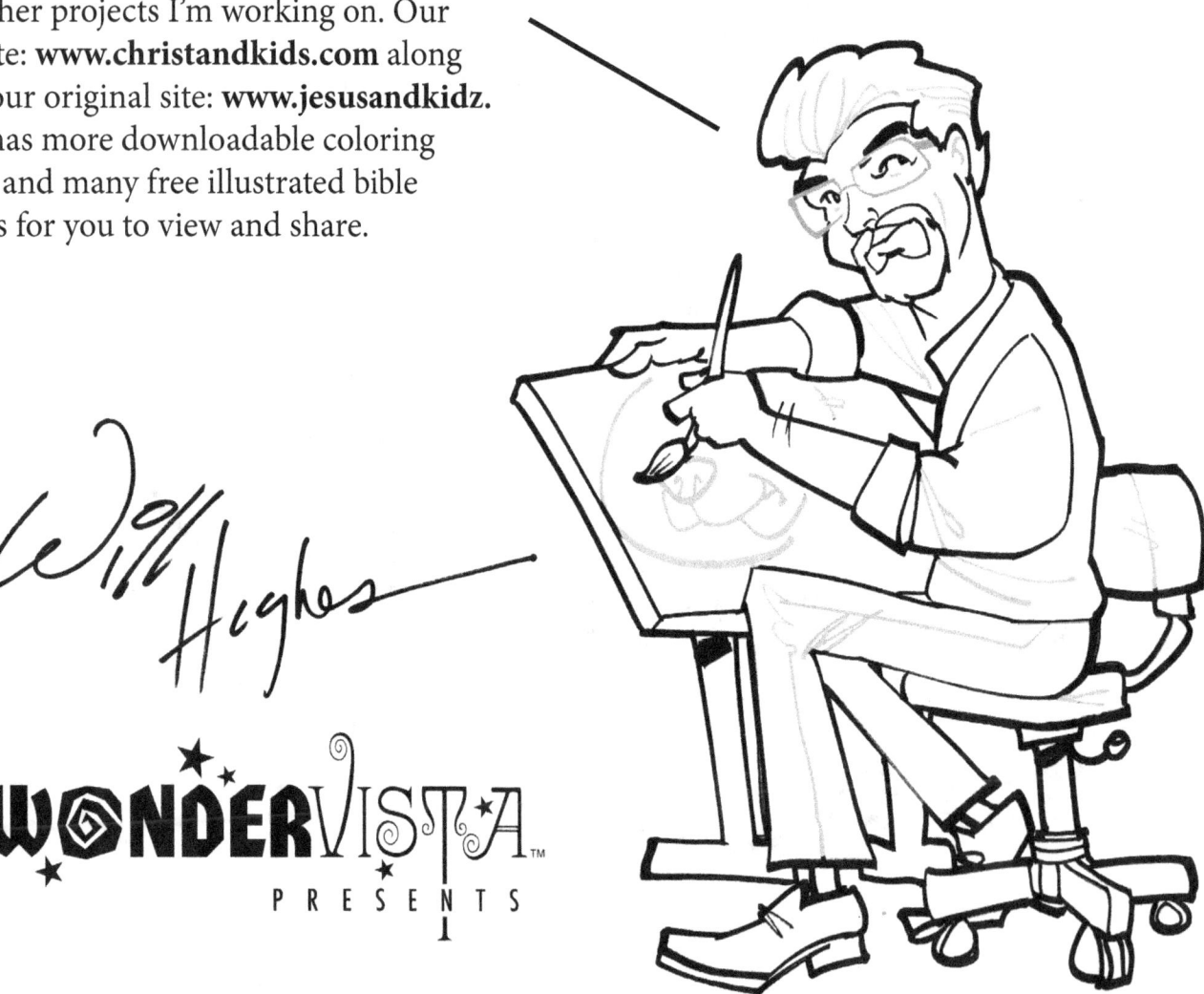

WONDERVISTA

PRESENTS

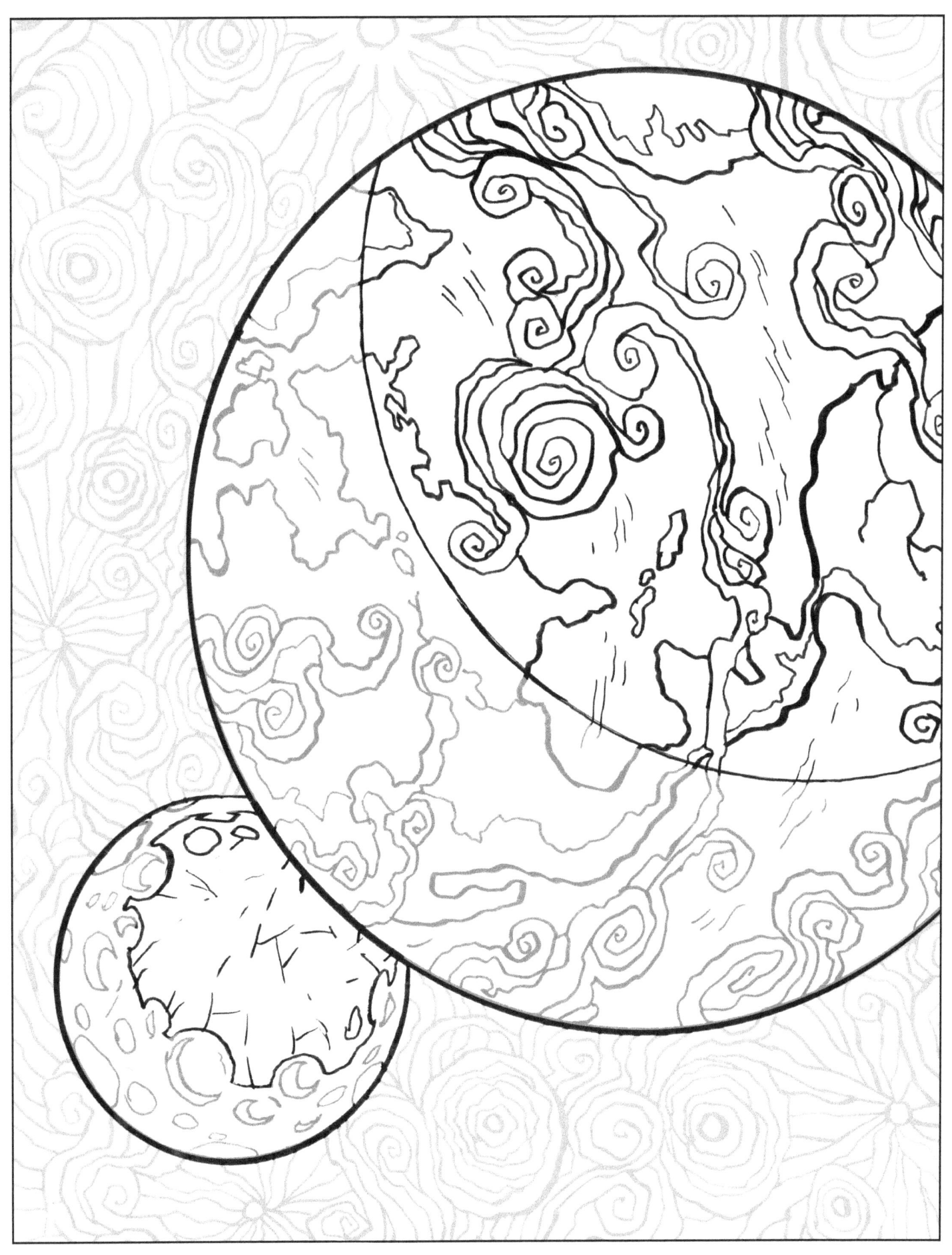

GOD CREATED THE HEAVEN AND THE EARTH

GENESIS 1
KING JAMES BIBLE

IN THE BEGINNING GOD CREATED THE HEAVEN AND THE EARTH.

AND THE EARTH WAS WITHOUT FORM, AND VOID; AND DARKNESS WAS UPON THE FACE OF THE DEEP. AND THE SPIRIT OF GOD MOVED UPON THE FACE OF THE WATERS.

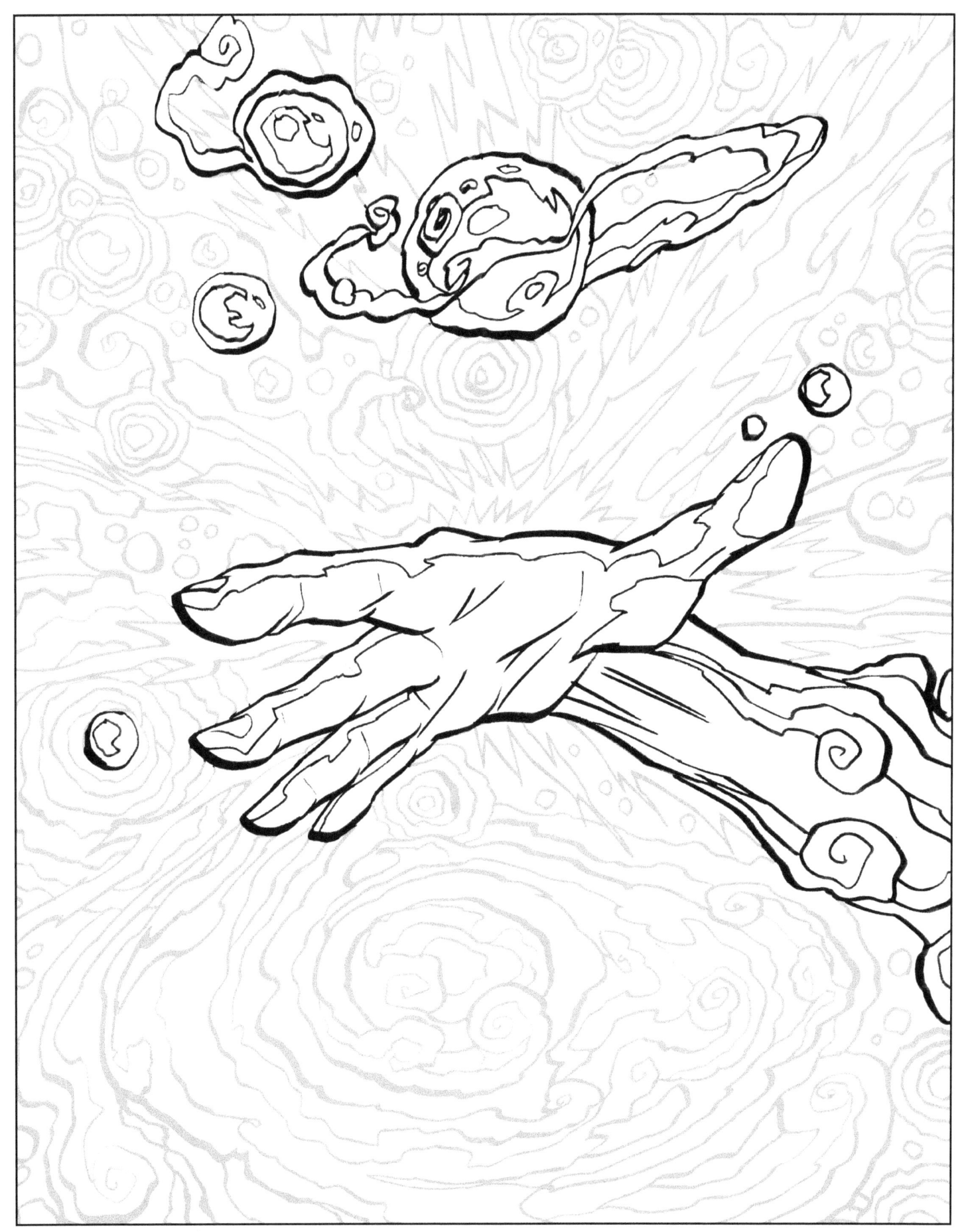

THE FIRST DAY: LIGHT

Genesis 1:3
King James Bible

And God said, Let there be light: and there was light.

And God saw the light, that it was good: and God divided the light from the darkness.

And God called the light Day, and the darkness he called Night. And the evening and the morning were the first day.

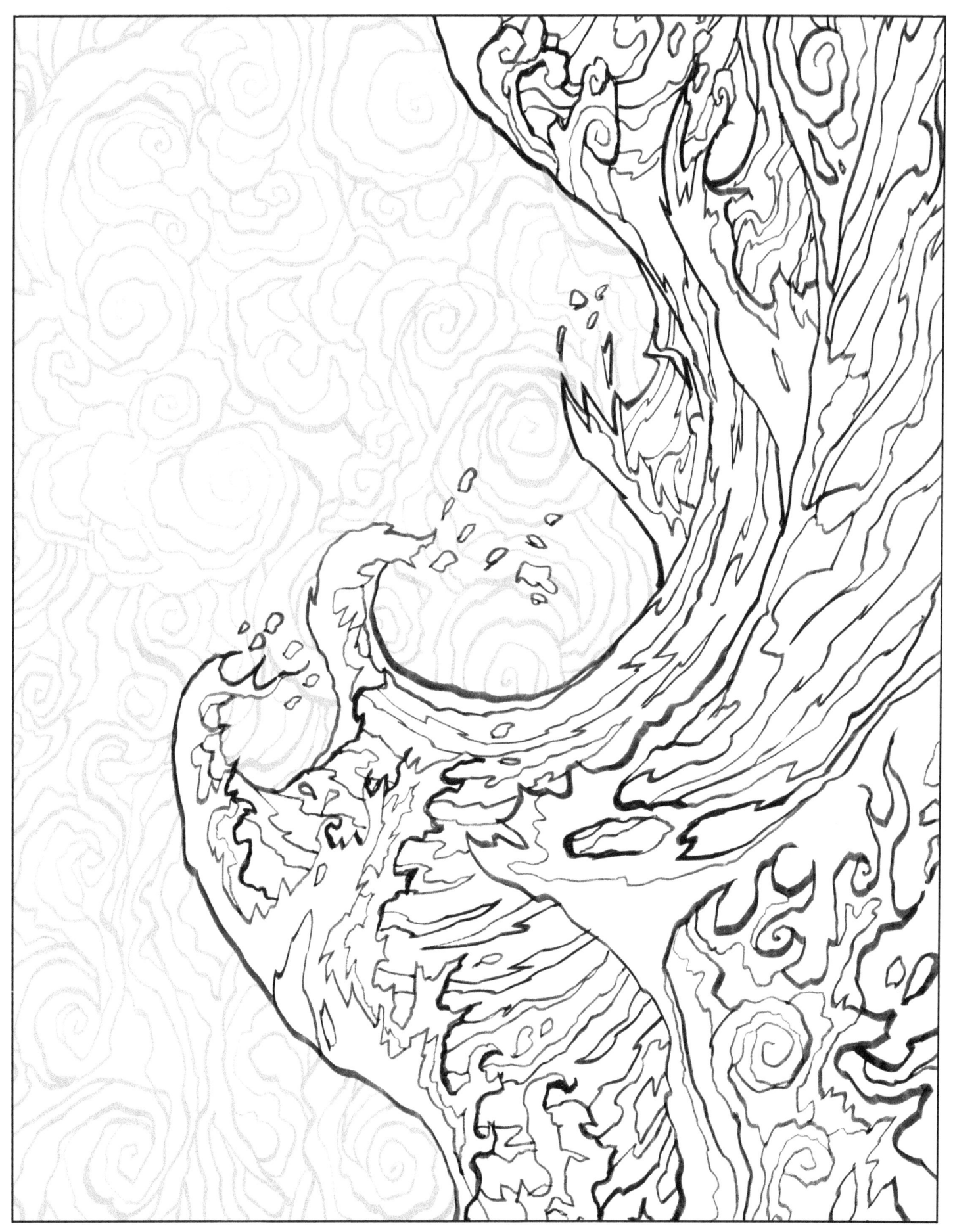

The Second Day: Dividing the Waters

GENESIS 1:6
KING JAMES BIBLE

AND GOD SAID, LET THERE BE A FIRMAMENT IN THE MIDST OF THE WATERS, AND LET IT DIVIDE THE WATERS FROM THE WATERS.

AND GOD MADE THE FIRMAMENT, AND DIVIDED THE WATERS WHICH WERE UNDER THE FIRMAMENT FROM THE WATERS WHICH WERE ABOVE THE FIRMAMENT: AND IT WAS SO.

AND GOD CALLED THE FIRMAMENT HEAVEN. AND THE EVENING AND THE MORNING WERE THE SECOND DAY.

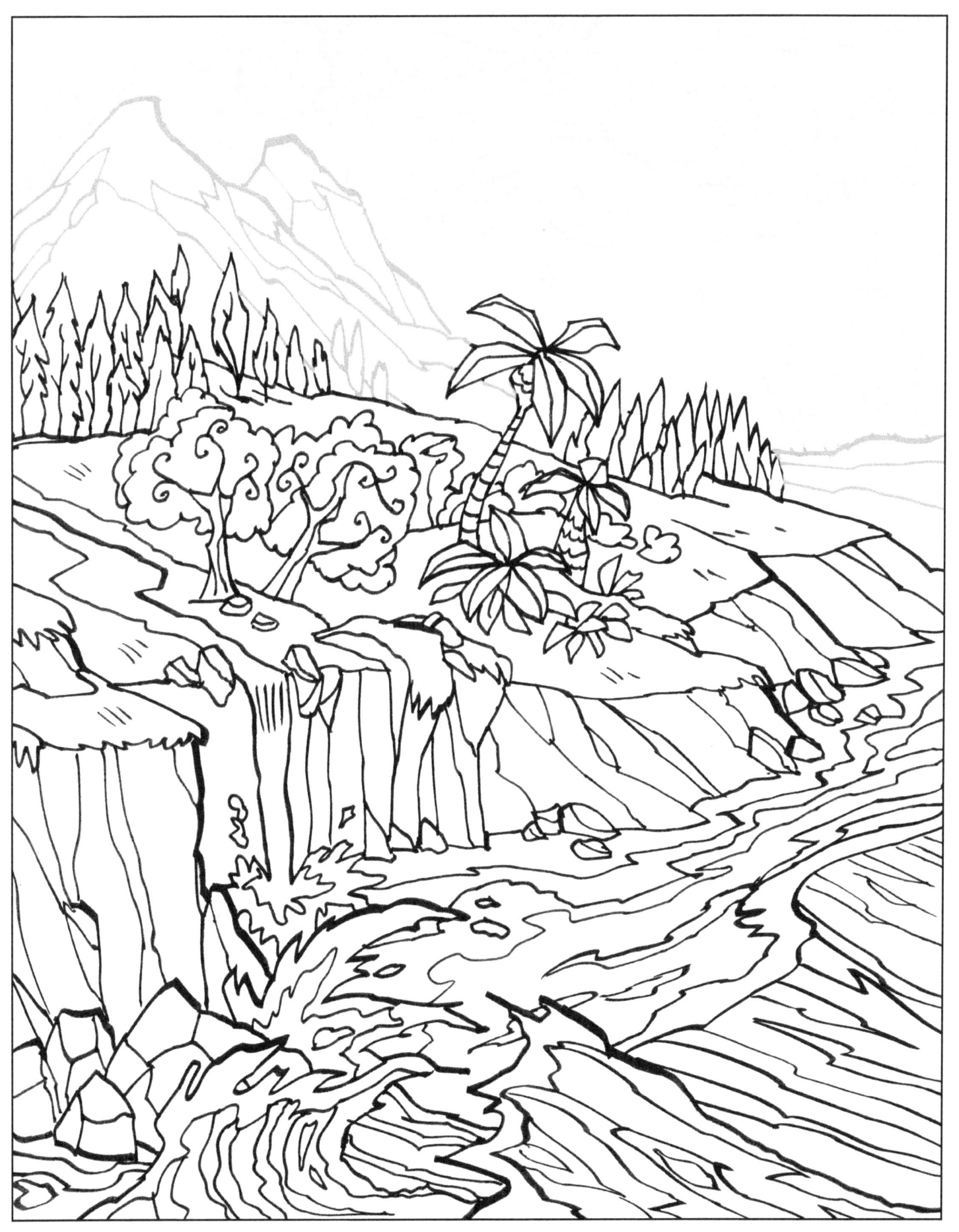

THE THIRD DAY BRINGING FORTH LAND FROM THE SEA

Genesis 1:9
King James Bible

And God said, Let the waters under the heaven be gathered together unto one place, and let the dry land appear: and it was so.

And God called the dry land Earth; and the gathering together of the waters called he Seas: and God saw that it was good.

And God said, Let the earth bring forth grass, the herb yielding seed, and the fruit tree yielding fruit after his kind, whose seed is in itself, upon the earth: and it was so.

And the earth brought forth grass, and herb yielding seed after his kind, and the tree yielding fruit, whose seed was in itself, after his kind: and God saw that it was good.

And the evening and the morning were the third day.

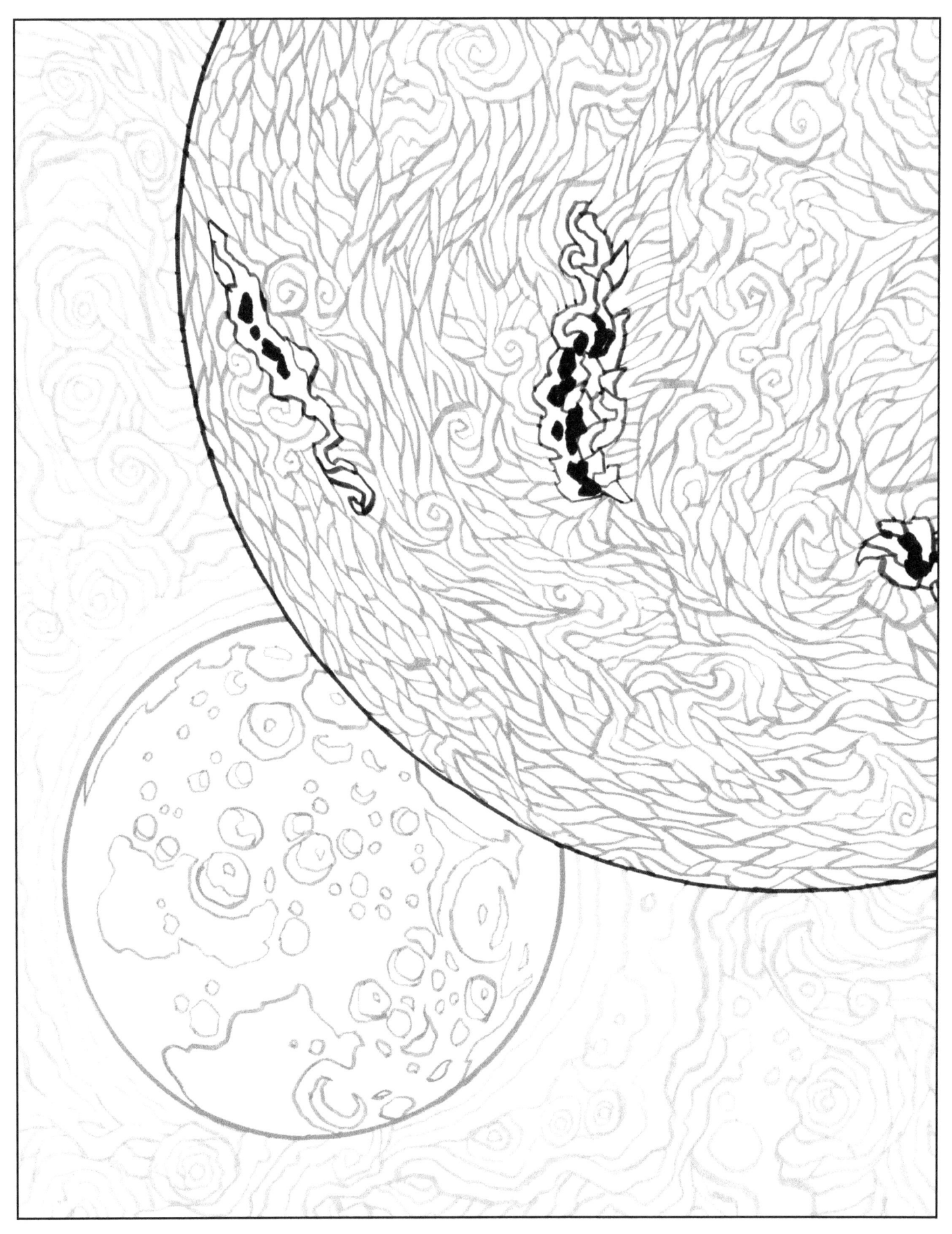

THE FOURTH DAY, LIGHTS IN THE FIRMAMENT OF HEAVEN

Genesis 1:14
King James Bible

And God said, Let there be lights in the firmament of the heaven to divide the day from the night; and let them be for signs, and for seasons, and for days, and years:

And let them be for lights in the firmament of the heaven to give light upon the earth: and it was so.

And God made two great lights; the greater light to rule the day, and the lesser light to rule the night: he made the stars also.

And God set them in the firmament of the heaven to give light upon the earth,

And to rule over the day and over the night, and to divide the light from the darkness: and God saw that it was good.

And the evening and the morning were the fourth day.

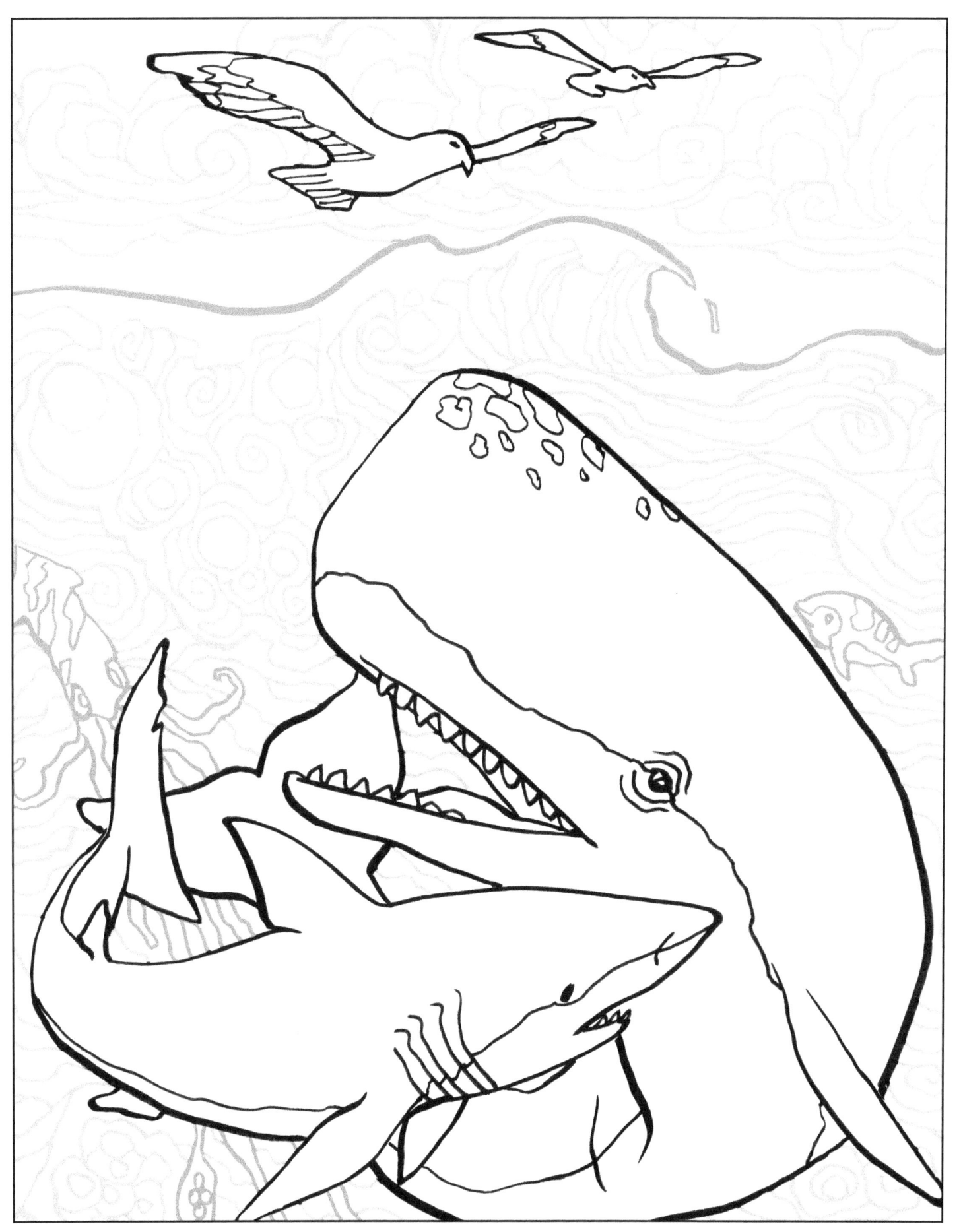

THE FIFTH DAY, GOD CREATED GREAT SEA CREATURES

Genesis 1:20
King James Bible

And God said, Let the waters bring forth abundantly the moving creature that hath life, and fowl that may fly above the earth in the open firmament of heaven.

And God created great whales, and every living creature that moveth, which the waters brought forth abundantly, after their kind, and every winged fowl after his kind: and God saw that it was good.

And God blessed them, saying, Be fruitful, and multiply, and fill the waters in the seas, and let fowl multiply in the earth.

And the evening and the morning were the fifth day.

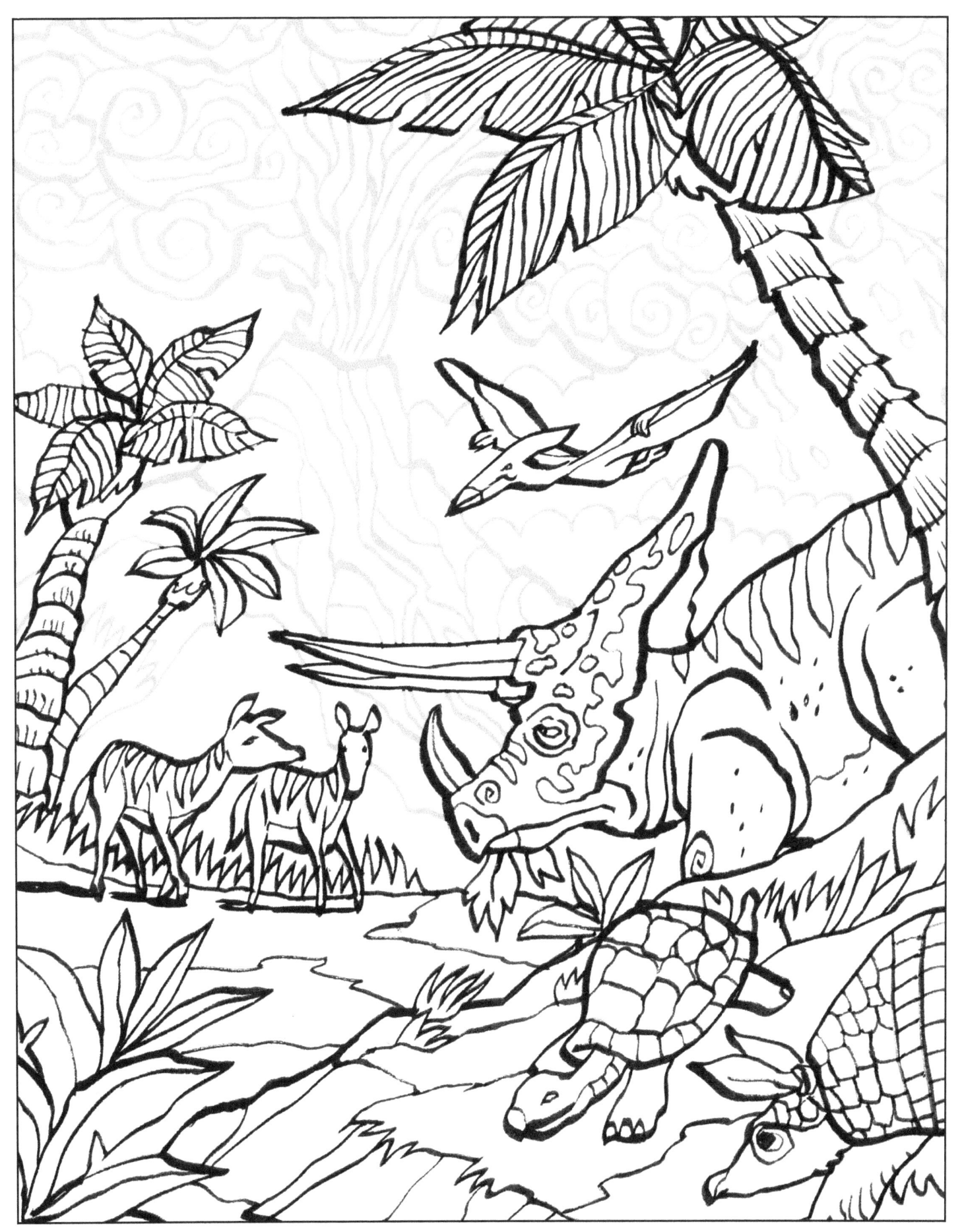

THE SIXTH DAY, GOD MADE THE BEASTS OF THE EARTH

Genesis 1:24

King James Bible

And God said, Let the earth bring forth the living creature after his kind, cattle, and creeping thing, and beast of the earth after his kind: and it was so.

And God made the beast of the earth after his kind, and cattle after their kind, and every thing that creepeth upon the earth after his kind: and God saw that it was good.

And God said, Let us make man in our image, after our likeness: and let them have dominion over the fish of the sea, and over the fowl of the air, and over the cattle, and over all the earth, and over every creeping thing that creepeth upon the earth.

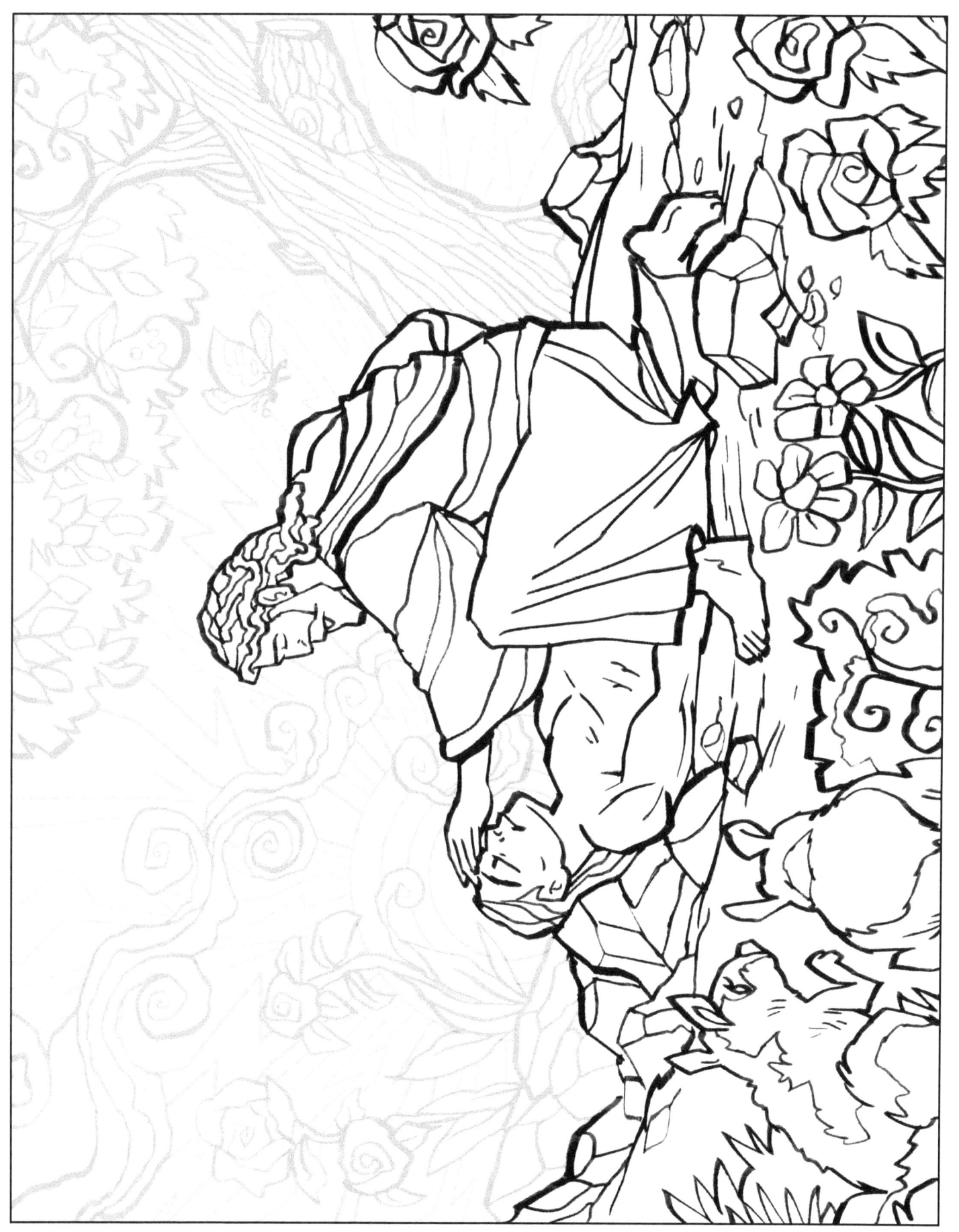

THEN GOD MADE MAN IN HIS OWN IMAGE

GENESIS 1:27
KING JAMES BIBLE

SO GOD CREATED MAN IN HIS OWN IMAGE, IN THE IMAGE OF GOD CREATED HE HIM...

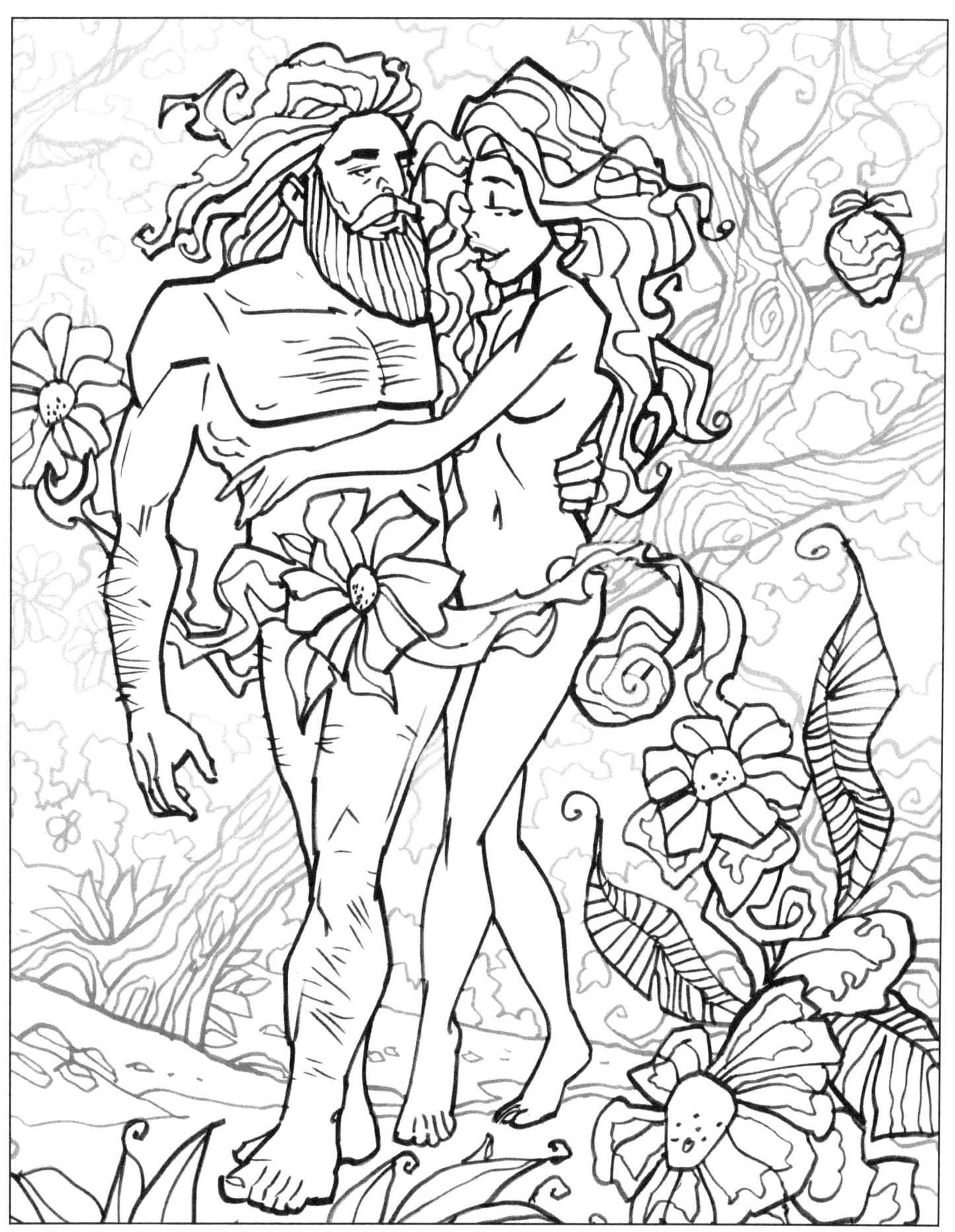

MALE AND FEMALE HE MADE THEM

Genesis 1:27 continued
King James Bible

...male and female created he them.

And God blessed them, and God said unto them, Be fruitful, and multiply, and replenish the earth, and subdue it: and have dominion over the fish of the sea, and over the fowl of the air, and over every living thing that moveth upon the earth.

And God said, Behold, I have given you every herb bearing seed, which is upon the face of all the earth, and every tree, in the which is the fruit of a tree yielding seed; to you it shall be for meat.

And to every beast of the earth, and to every fowl of the air, and to every thing that creepeth upon the earth, wherein there is life, I have given every green herb for meat: and it was so.

And God saw every thing that he had made, and, behold, it was very good. And the evening and the morning were the sixth day

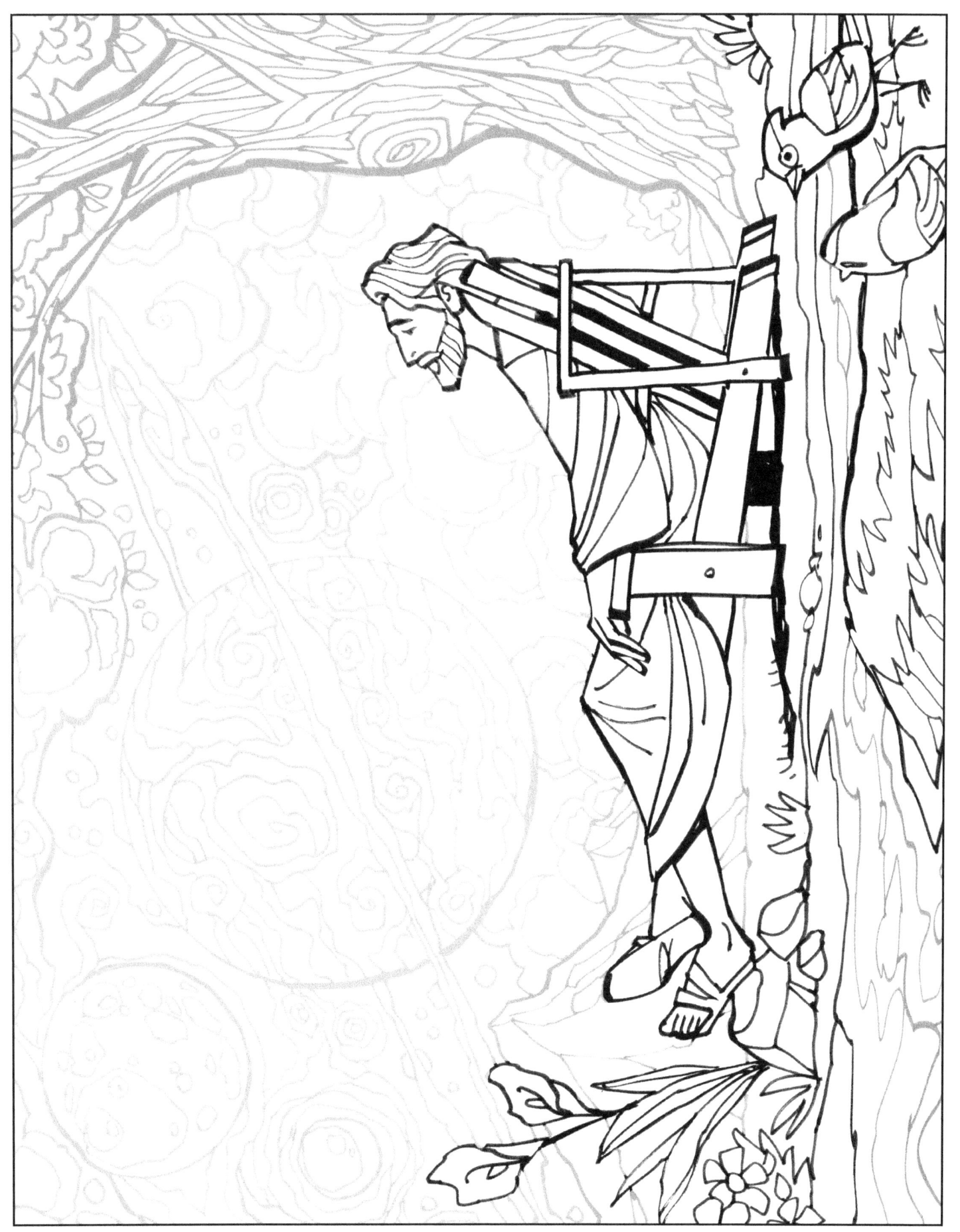

THE SEVENTH DAY: REST

GENESIS 2:1
KING JAMES BIBLE

THUS THE HEAVENS AND THE EARTH WERE FINISHED, AND ALL THE HOST OF THEM.

AND ON THE SEVENTH DAY GOD ENDED HIS WORK WHICH HE HAD MADE; AND HE RESTED ON THE SEVENTH DAY FROM ALL HIS WORK WHICH HE HAD MADE.

AND GOD BLESSED THE SEVENTH DAY, AND SANCTIFIED IT: BECAUSE THAT IN IT HE HAD RESTED FROM ALL HIS WORK WHICH GOD CREATED AND MADE.

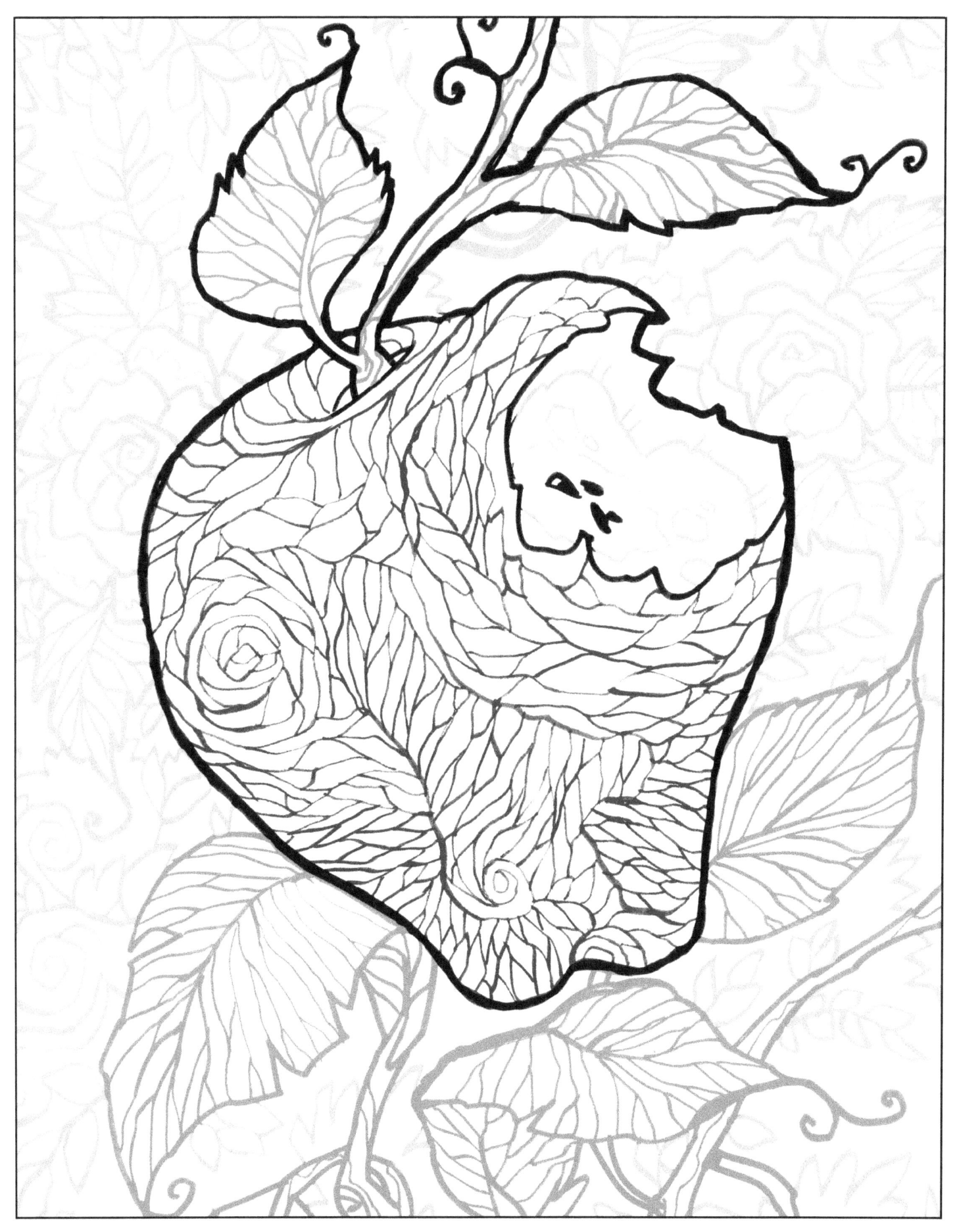

THE FRUIT OF THE TREE OF KNOWLEDGE

GENESIS 2:15
KING JAMES BIBLE

AND THE LORD GOD TOOK THE MAN, AND PUT HIM INTO THE GARDEN OF EDEN TO DRESS IT AND TO KEEP IT.

AND THE LORD GOD COMMANDED THE MAN, SAYING, OF EVERY TREE OF THE GARDEN THOU MAYEST FREELY EAT:

BUT OF THE TREE OF THE KNOWLEDGE OF GOOD AND EVIL, THOU SHALT NOT EAT OF IT: FOR IN THE DAY THAT THOU EATEST THEREOF THOU SHALT SURELY DIE.

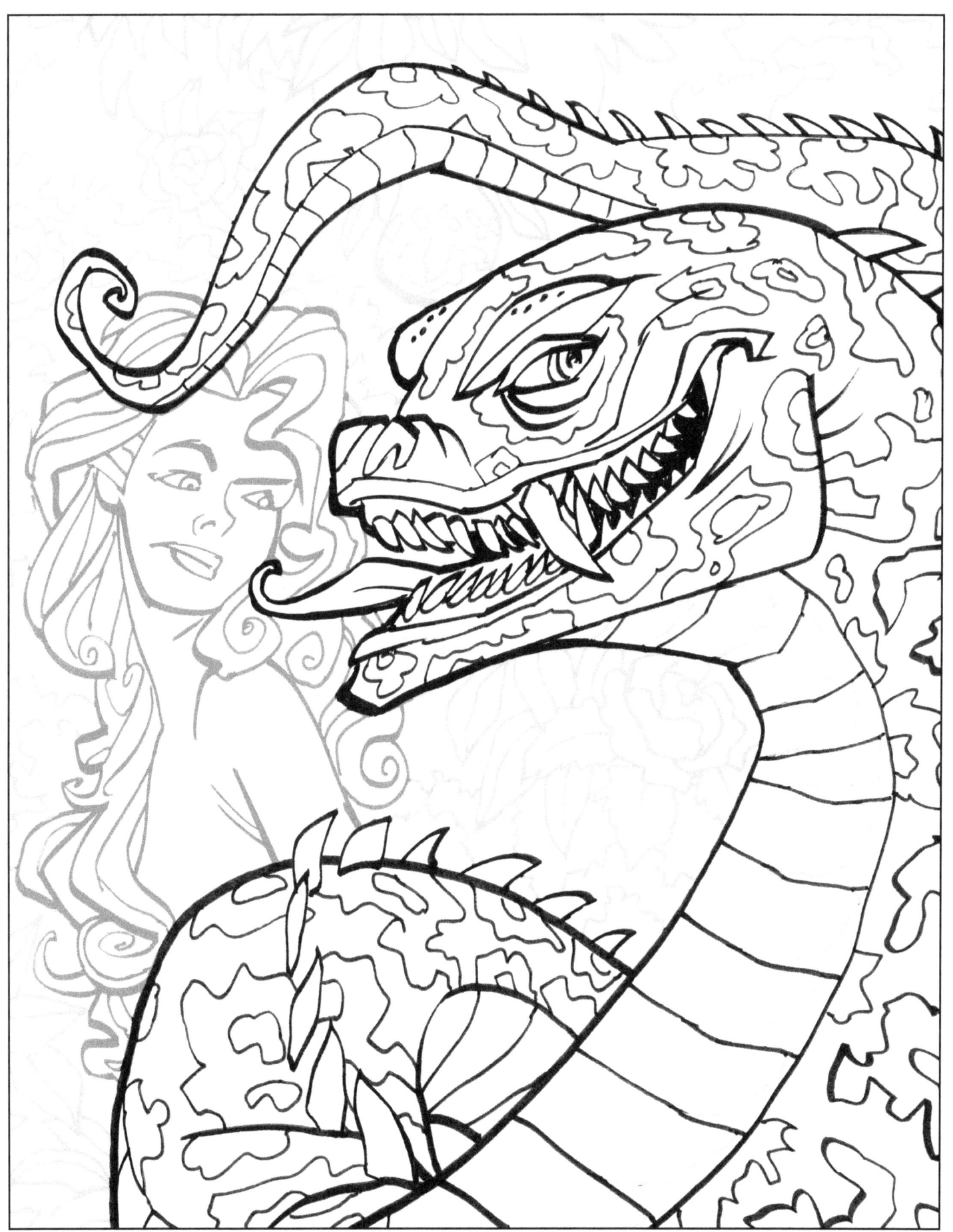

THE SERPENT

GENESIS 3:1
KING JAMES BIBLE

NOW THE SERPENT WAS MORE SUBTIL THAN ANY BEAST OF THE FIELD WHICH THE LORD GOD HAD MADE. AND HE SAID UNTO THE WOMAN, YEA, HATH GOD SAID, YE SHALL NOT EAT OF EVERY TREE OF THE GARDEN?

AND THE WOMAN SAID UNTO THE SERPENT, WE MAY EAT OF THE FRUIT OF THE TREES OF THE GARDEN:

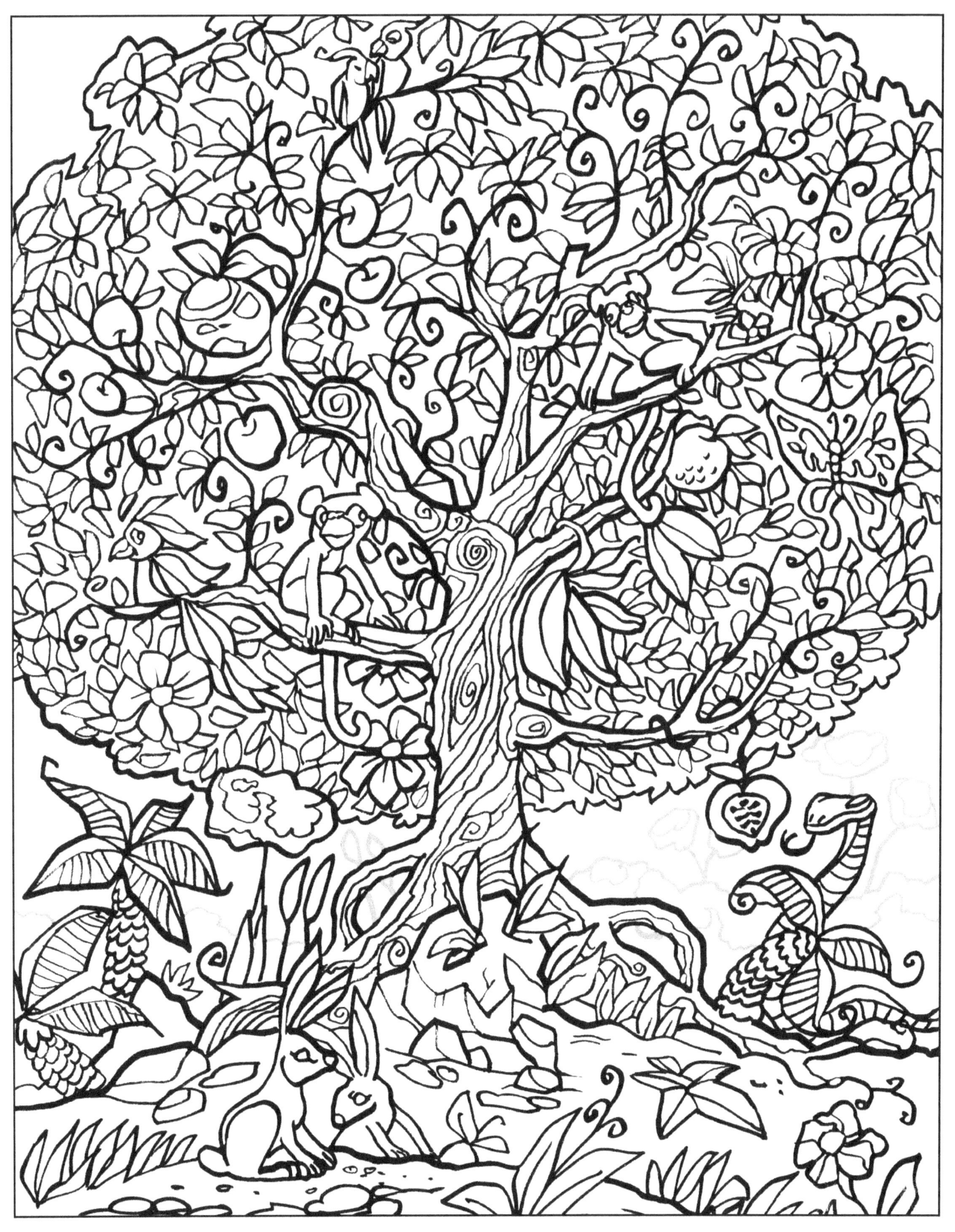

THE TREE OF THE KNOWLEDGE OF GOOD AND EVIL

Genesis 3:3
King James Bible

But of the fruit of the tree which is in the midst of the garden, God hath said, Ye shall not eat of it, neither shall ye touch it, lest ye die.

And the serpent said unto the woman, Ye shall not surely die:

For God doth know that in the day ye eat thereof, then your eyes shall be opened, and ye shall be as gods, knowing good and evil.

And when the woman saw that the tree was good for food, and that it was pleasant to the eyes, and a tree to be desired to make one wise, she took of the fruit thereof, and did eat, and gave also unto her husband with her; and he did eat.

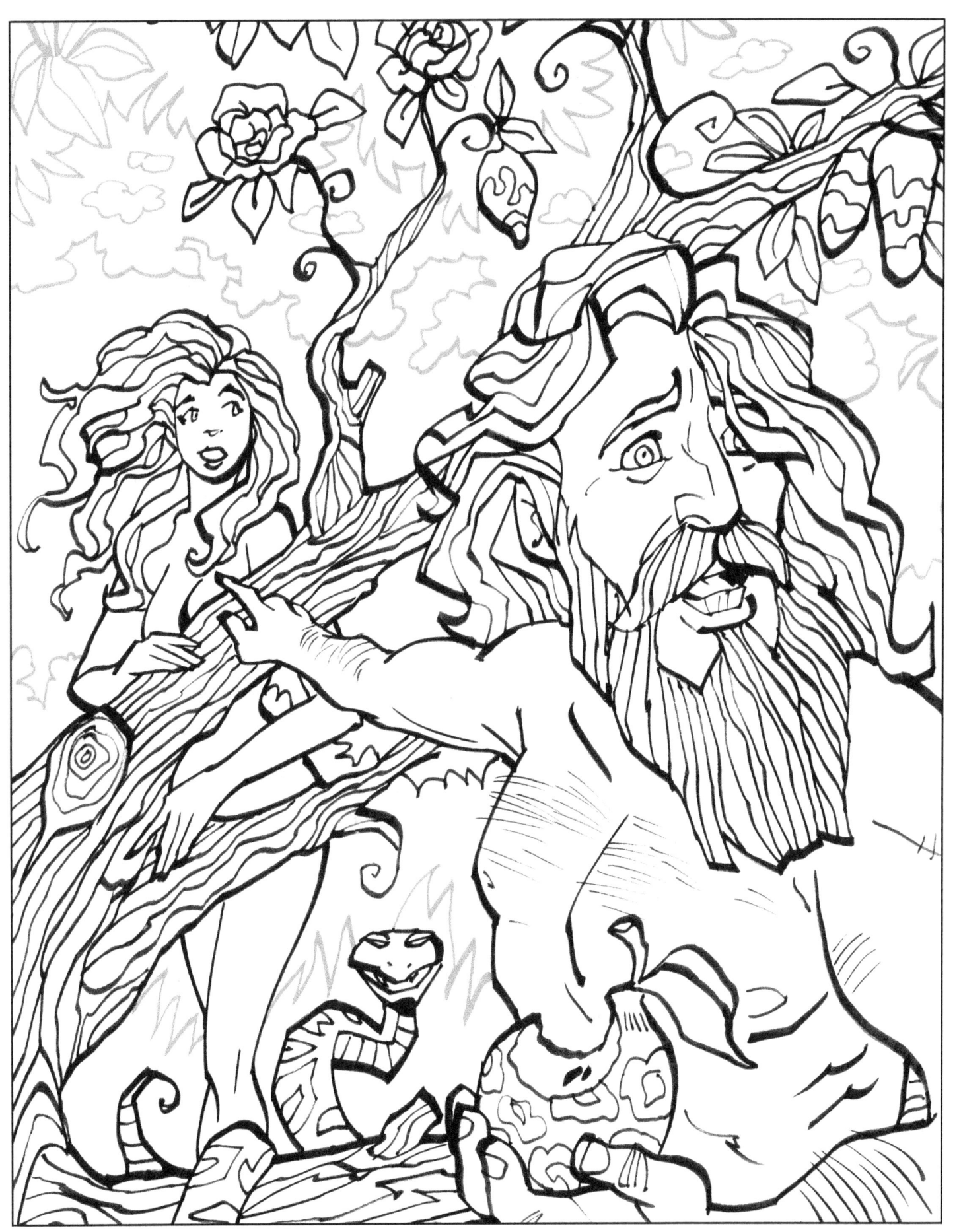

"THE WOMAN WHOM THOU GAVEST TO BE WITH ME,
SHE GAVE ME OF THE TREE, AND I DID EAT."

GENESIS 3:7
KING JAMES BIBLE

AND THE EYES OF THEM BOTH WERE OPENED, AND THEY KNEW THAT THEY WERE NAKED; AND THEY SEWED FIG LEAVES TOGETHER, AND MADE THEMSELVES APRONS.

AND THEY HEARD THE VOICE OF THE LORD GOD WALKING IN THE GARDEN IN THE COOL OF THE DAY: AND ADAM AND HIS WIFE HID THEMSELVES FROM THE PRESENCE OF THE LORD GOD AMONGST THE TREES OF THE GARDEN.

AND THE LORD GOD CALLED UNTO ADAM, AND SAID UNTO HIM, WHERE ART THOU?

AND HE SAID, I HEARD THY VOICE IN THE GARDEN, AND I WAS AFRAID, BECAUSE I WAS NAKED; AND I HID MYSELF.

AND HE SAID, WHO TOLD THEE THAT THOU WAST NAKED? HAST THOU EATEN OF THE TREE, WHEREOF I COMMANDED THEE THAT THOU SHOULDEST NOT EAT?

AND THE MAN SAID, THE WOMAN WHOM THOU GAVEST TO BE WITH ME, SHE GAVE ME OF THE TREE, AND I DID EAT.

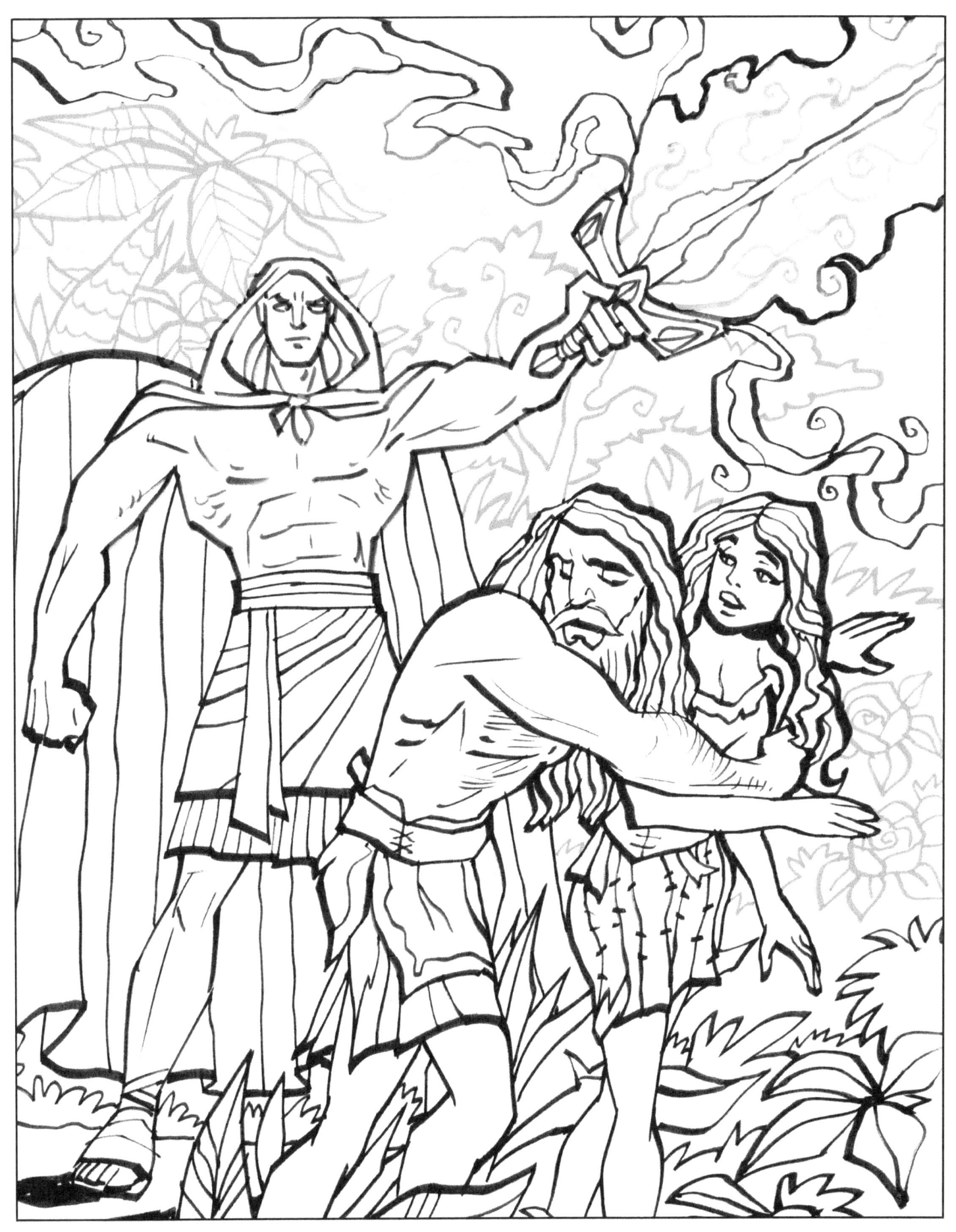

AND HE PLACED AT THE EAST OF THE GARDEN OF EDEN CHERUBIMS

Genesis 3:21
King James Bible

Unto Adam also and to his wife did the Lord God make coats of skins, and clothed them.

And the Lord God said, Behold, the man is become as one of us, to know good and evil: and now, lest he put forth his hand, and take also of the tree of life, and eat, and live for ever:

Therefore the Lord God sent him forth from the garden of Eden, to till the ground from whence he was taken.

So he drove out the man; and he placed at the east of the garden of Eden Cherubims, and a flaming sword which turned every way, to keep the way of the tree of life.

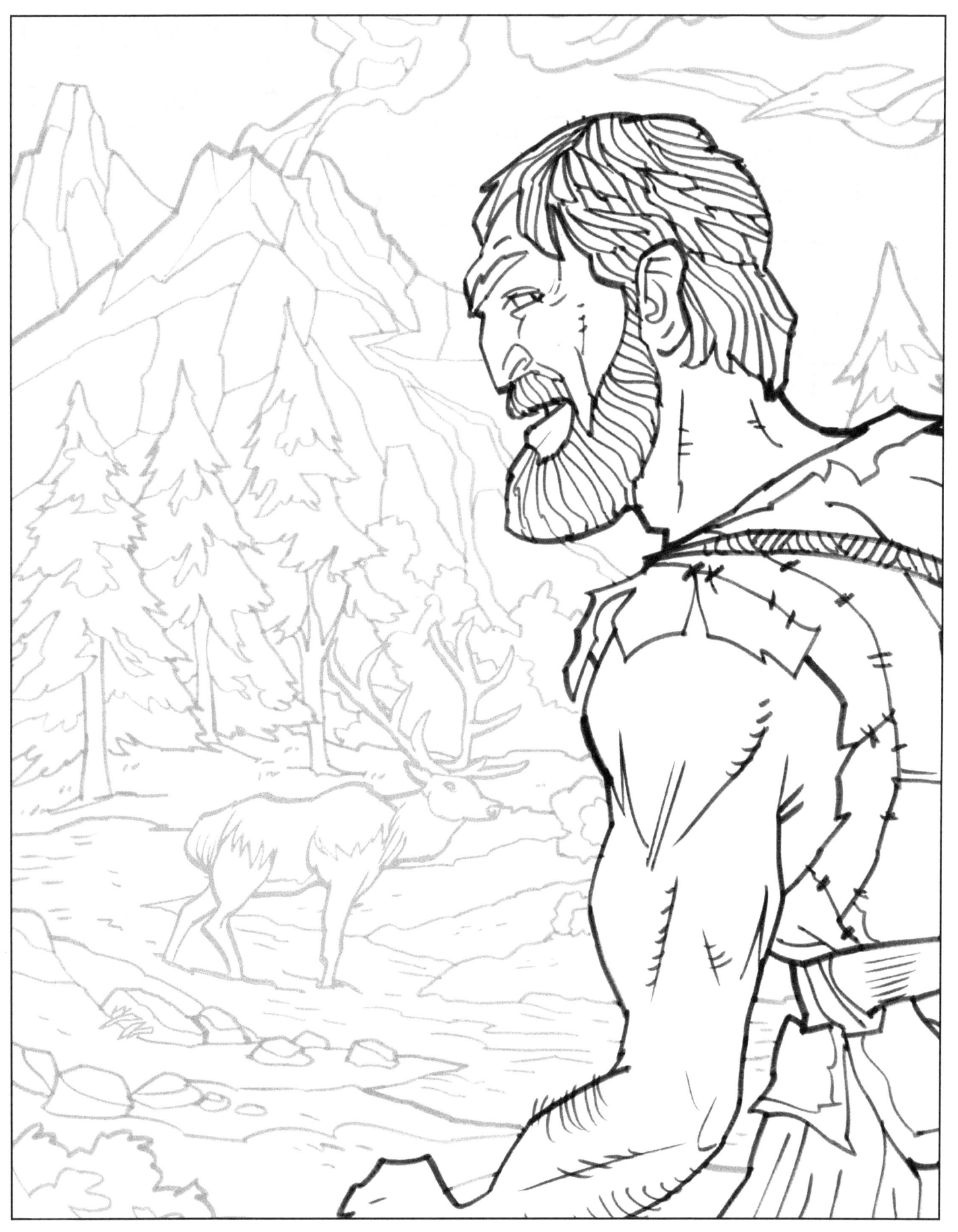

THE LAND OF NOD, ON THE EAST OF EDEN

Genesis 4:14

King James Bible
After Cain Kills His Brother Able...

Behold, thou hast driven me out this day from the face of the earth; and from thy face shall I be hid; and I shall be a fugitive and a vagabond in the earth; and it shall come to pass, that every one that findeth me shall slay me.

And the Lord said unto him, Therefore whosoever slayeth Cain, vengeance shall be taken on him sevenfold. And the Lord set a mark upon Cain, lest any finding him should kill him.

And Cain went out from the presence of the Lord, and dwelt in the land of Nod, on the east of Eden

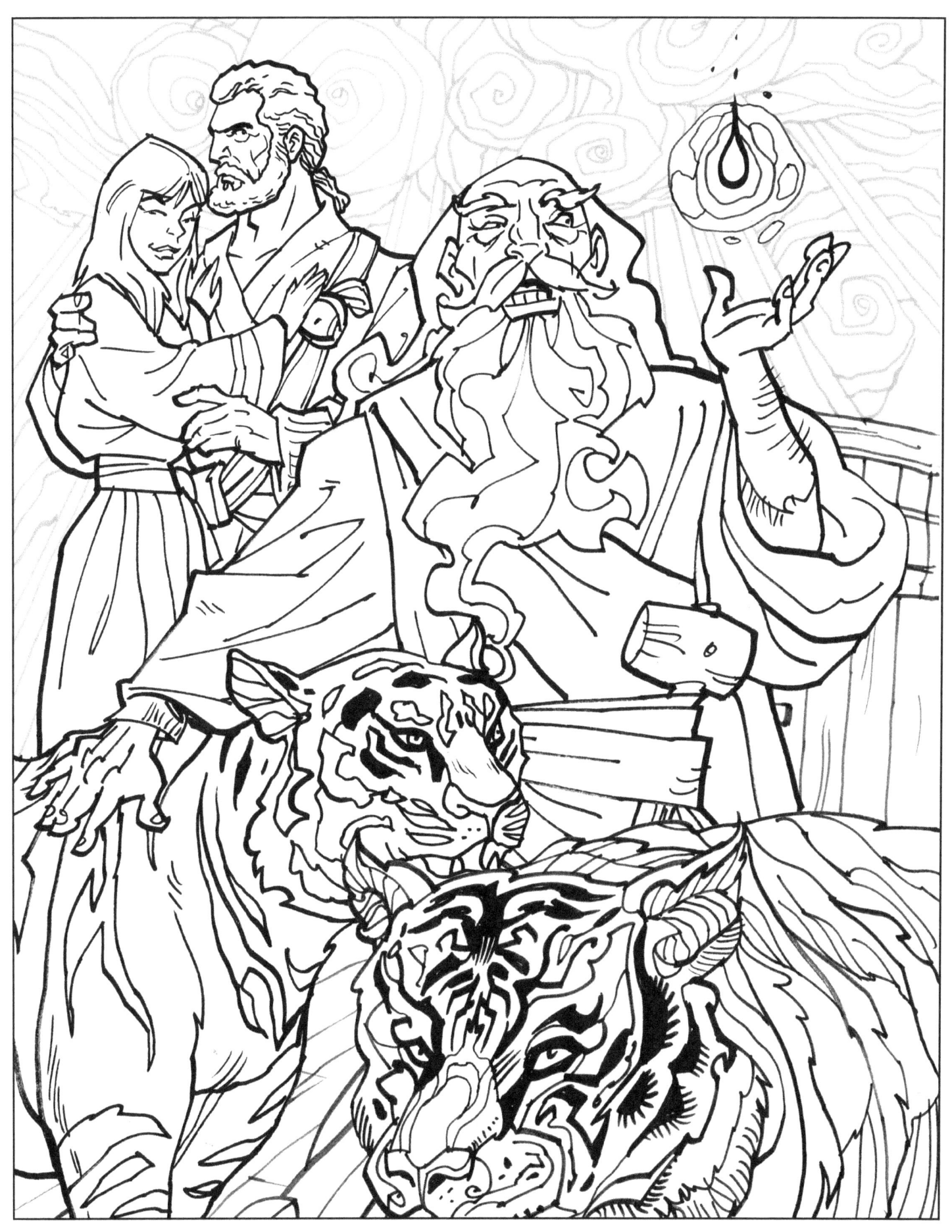

NOAH FOUND GRACE IN THE EYES OF THE LORD

Genesis 6:5

King James Bible

And God saw that the wickedness of man was great in the earth, and that every imagination of the thoughts of his heart was only evil continually.

And it repented the Lord that he had made man on the earth, and it grieved him at his heart.

And the Lord said, I will destroy man whom I have created from the face of the earth; both man, and beast, and the creeping thing, and the fowls of the air; for it repenteth me that I have made them.

But Noah found grace in the eyes of the Lord.

These are the generations of Noah: Noah was a just man and perfect in his generations, and Noah walked with God.

And Noah begat three sons, Shem, Ham, and Japheth.

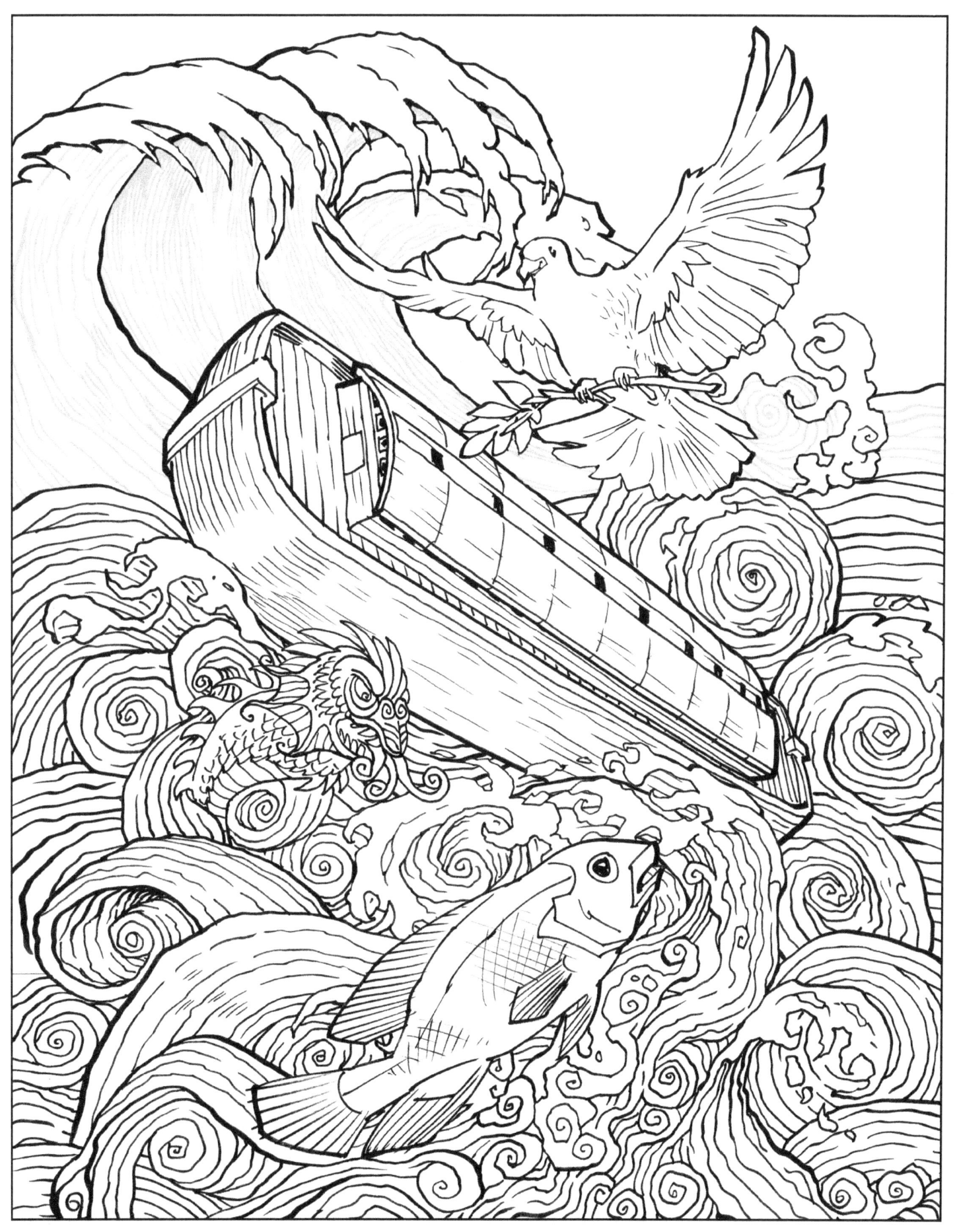

Come Thou and All Thy House into the Ark

Genesis 7:1
King James Bible

And the Lord said unto Noah, Come thou and all thy house into the ark; for thee have I seen righteous before me in this generation.

Of every clean beast thou shalt take to thee by sevens, the male and his female: and of beasts that are not clean by two, the male and his female.

Of fowls also of the air by sevens, the male and the female; to keep seed alive upon the face of all the earth.

For yet seven days, and I will cause it to rain upon the earth forty days and forty nights; and every living substance that I have made will I destroy from off the face of the earth.

And Noah did according unto all that the Lord commanded him.

And Noah was six hundred years old when the flood of waters was upon the earth.

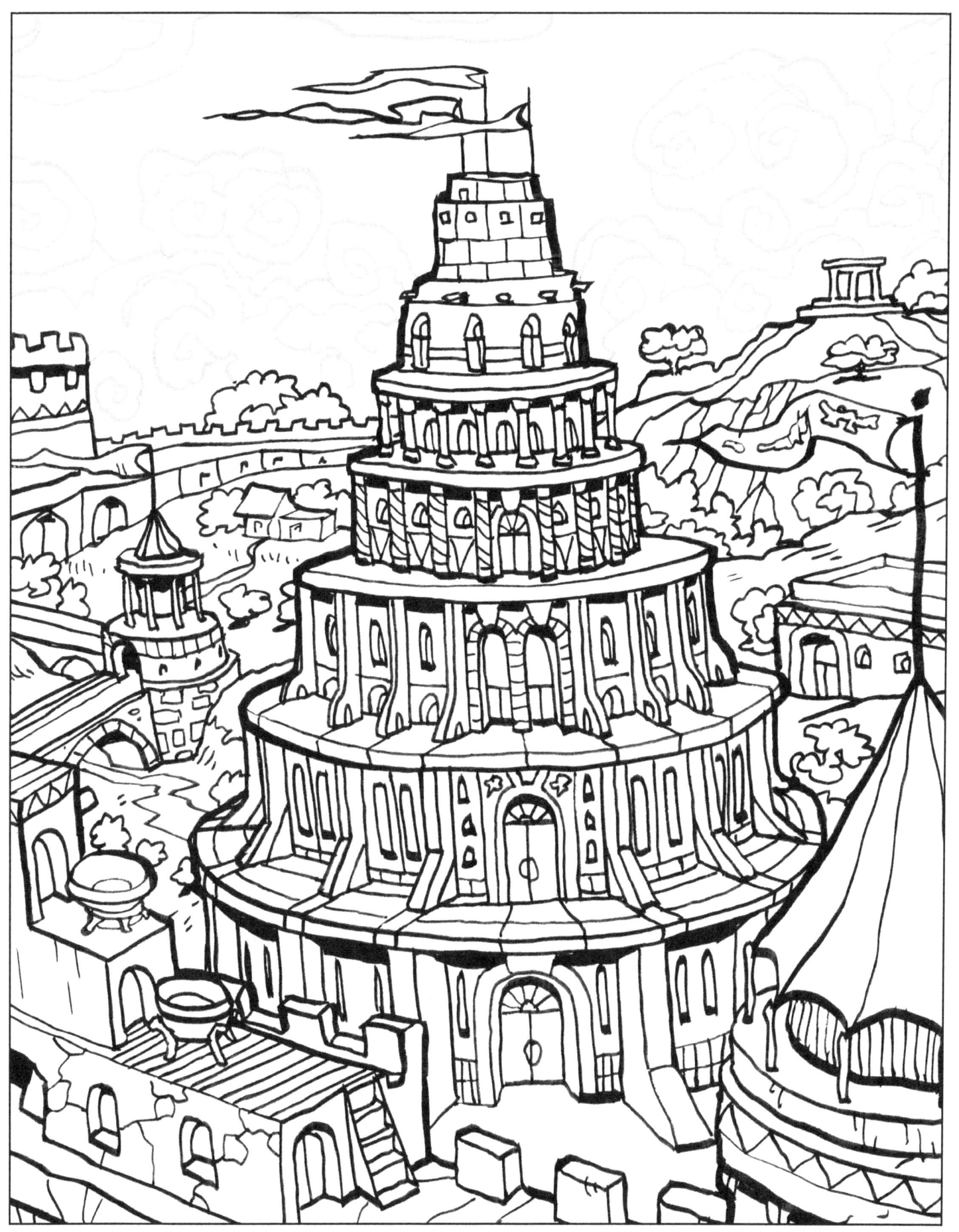

THE TOWER OF BABEL

GENESIS 11:1
KING JAMES BIBLE

AND THE WHOLE EARTH WAS OF ONE LANGUAGE, AND OF ONE SPEECH.

AND IT CAME TO PASS, AS THEY JOURNEYED FROM THE EAST, THAT THEY FOUND A PLAIN IN THE LAND OF SHINAR; AND THEY DWELT THERE.

AND THEY SAID ONE TO ANOTHER, GO TO, LET US MAKE BRICK, AND BURN THEM THOROUGHLY. AND THEY HAD BRICK FOR STONE, AND SLIME HAD THEY FOR MORTER.

AND THEY SAID, GO TO, LET US BUILD US A CITY AND A TOWER, WHOSE TOP MAY REACH UNTO HEAVEN; AND LET US MAKE US A NAME, LEST WE BE SCATTERED ABROAD UPON THE FACE OF THE WHOLE EARTH.

AND THE LORD CAME DOWN TO SEE THE CITY AND THE TOWER, WHICH THE CHILDREN OF MEN BUILDED.

AND THE LORD SAID, BEHOLD, THE PEOPLE IS ONE, AND THEY HAVE ALL ONE LANGUAGE; AND THIS THEY BEGIN TO DO: AND NOW NOTHING WILL BE RESTRAINED FROM THEM, WHICH THEY HAVE IMAGINED TO DO.

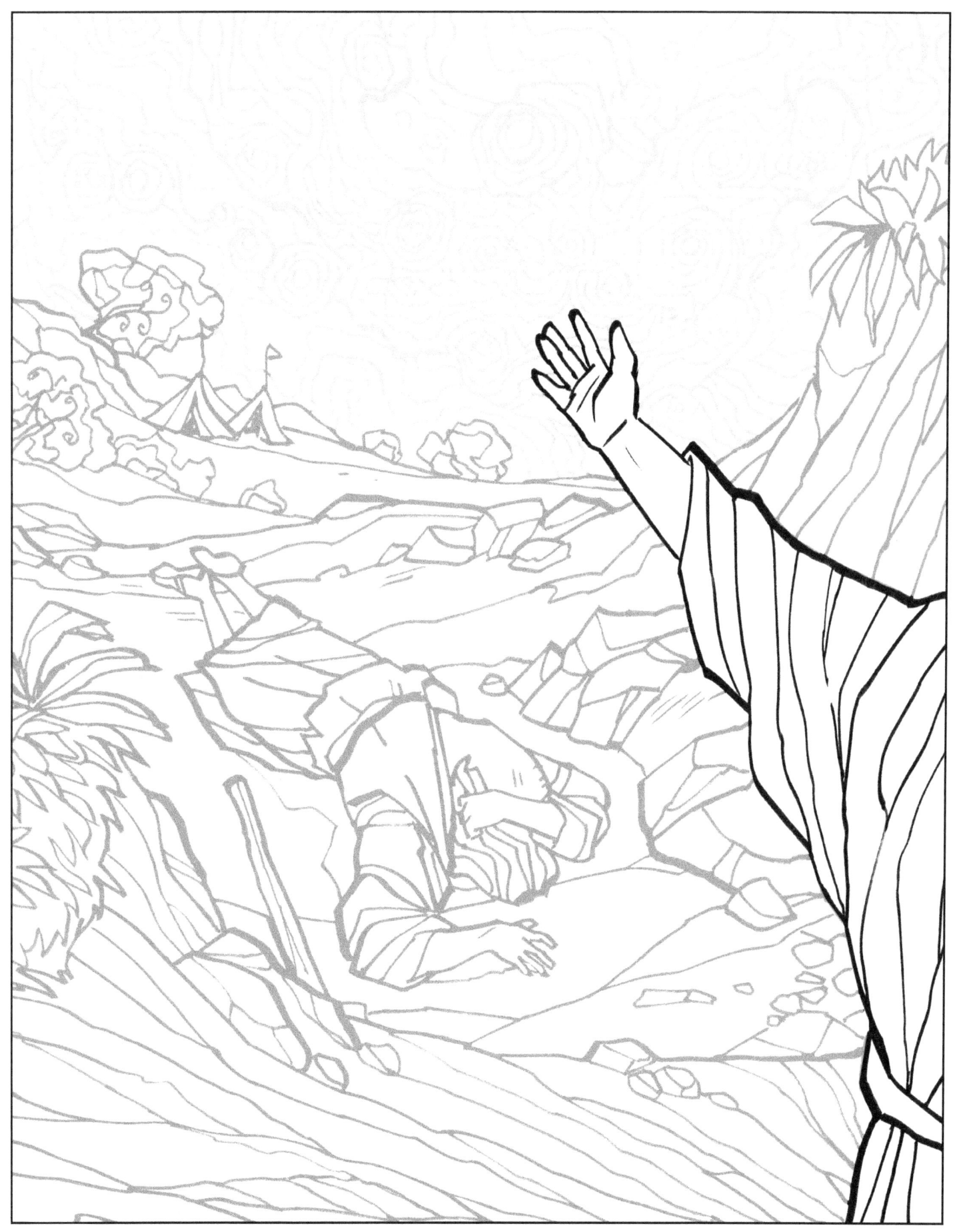

GOD'S COVENANT WITH ABRAHAM

GENESIS 17:1

KING JAMES BIBLE

AND WHEN ABRAM WAS NINETY YEARS OLD AND NINE, THE LORD APPEARED TO ABRAM, AND SAID UNTO HIM, I AM THE ALMIGHTY GOD; WALK BEFORE ME, AND BE THOU PERFECT.

AND I WILL MAKE MY COVENANT BETWEEN ME AND THEE, AND WILL MULTIPLY THEE EXCEEDINGLY.

AND ABRAM FELL ON HIS FACE: AND GOD TALKED WITH HIM, SAYING,

AS FOR ME, BEHOLD, MY COVENANT IS WITH THEE, AND THOU SHALT BE A FATHER OF MANY NATIONS.

NEITHER SHALL THY NAME ANY MORE BE CALLED ABRAM, BUT THY NAME SHALL BE ABRAHAM; FOR A FATHER OF MANY NATIONS HAVE I MADE THEE.

AND I WILL MAKE THEE EXCEEDING FRUITFUL, AND I WILL MAKE NATIONS OF THEE, AND KINGS SHALL COME OUT OF THEE.

AND I WILL ESTABLISH MY COVENANT BETWEEN ME AND THEE AND THY SEED AFTER THEE IN THEIR GENERATIONS FOR AN EVERLASTING COVENANT, TO BE A GOD UNTO THEE, AND TO THY SEED AFTER THEE.

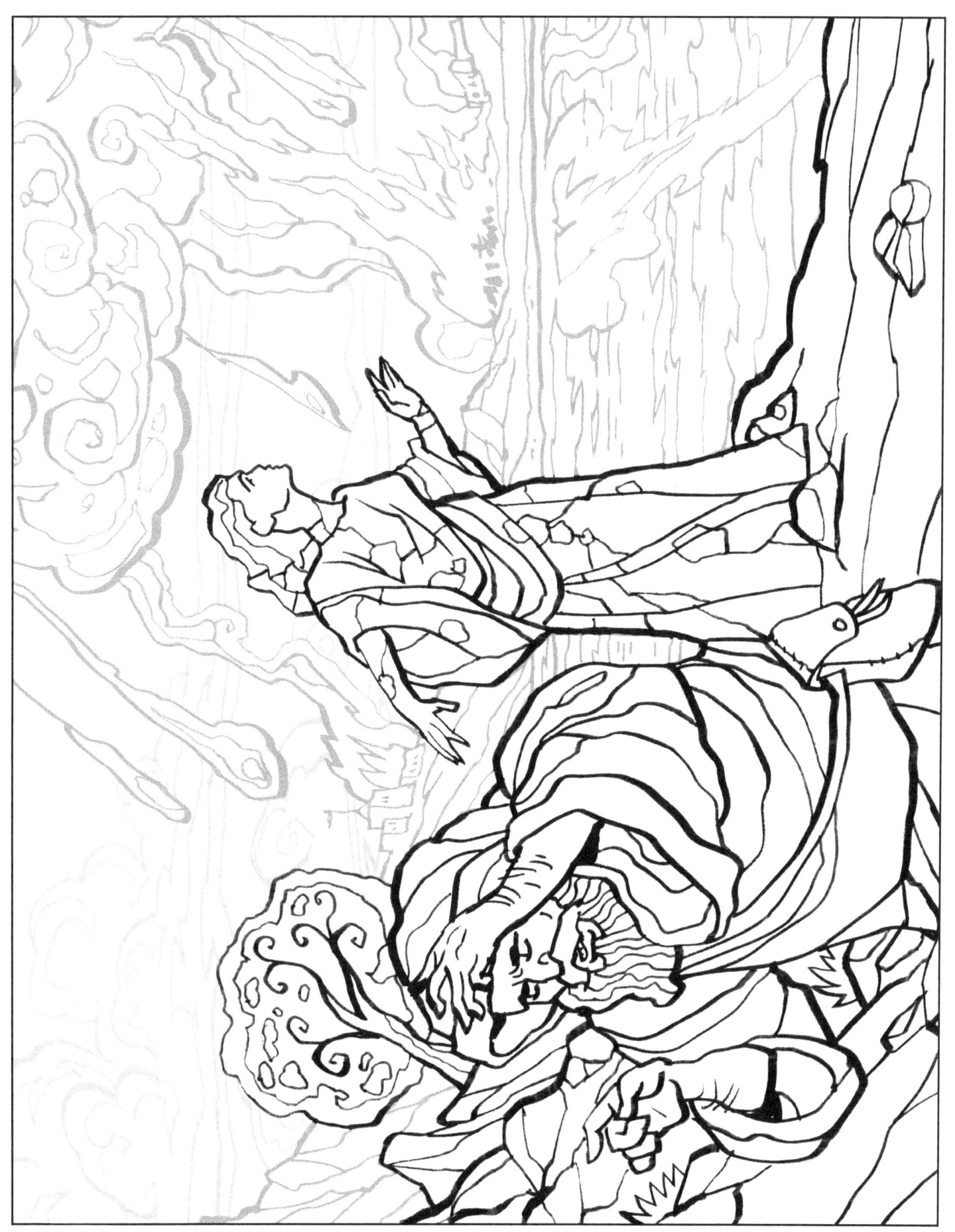

BRIMSTONE AND FIRE FROM THE LORD

Genesis 19:24
King James Bible

Then the Lord rained upon Sodom and upon Gomorrah brimstone and fire from the Lord out of heaven;

And he overthrew those cities, and all the plain, and all the inhabitants of the cities, and that which grew upon the ground.

But his wife looked back from behind him, and she became a pillar of salt.

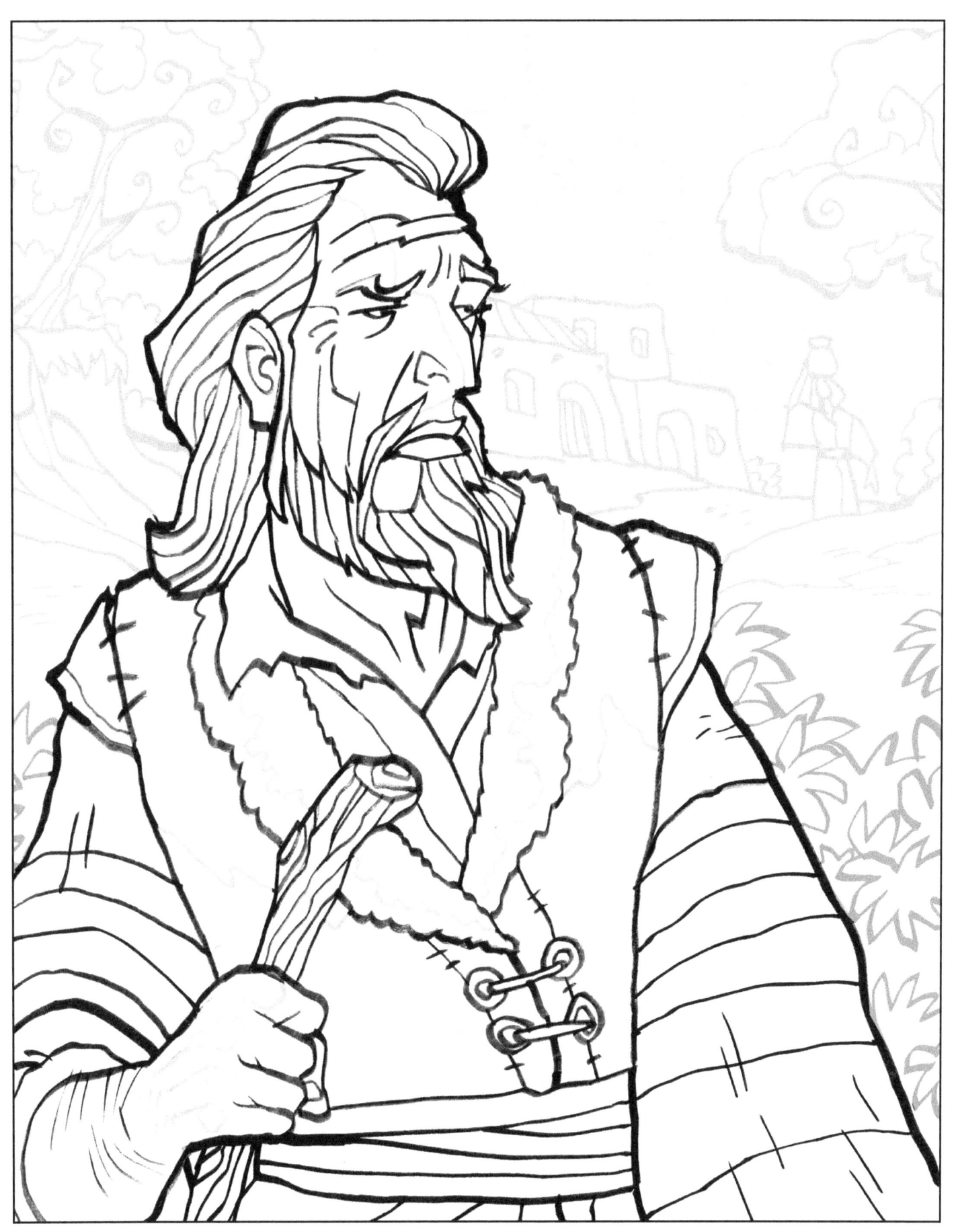

GOD FULFILLS HIS PROMISE TO ABRAHAM

Genesis 21:1

King James Bible

And the Lord visited Sarah as he had said, and the Lord did unto Sarah as he had spoken.

For Sarah conceived, and bare Abraham a son in his old age, at the set time of which God had spoken to him.

And Abraham called the name of his son that was born unto him, whom Sarah bare to him, Isaac.

Genesis 22:1

And it came to pass after these things, that God did tempt Abraham, and said unto him, Abraham: and he said, Behold, here I am.

And he said, Take now thy son, thine only son Isaac, whom thou lovest, and get thee into the land of Moriah; and offer him there for a burnt offering upon one of the mountains which I will tell thee of.

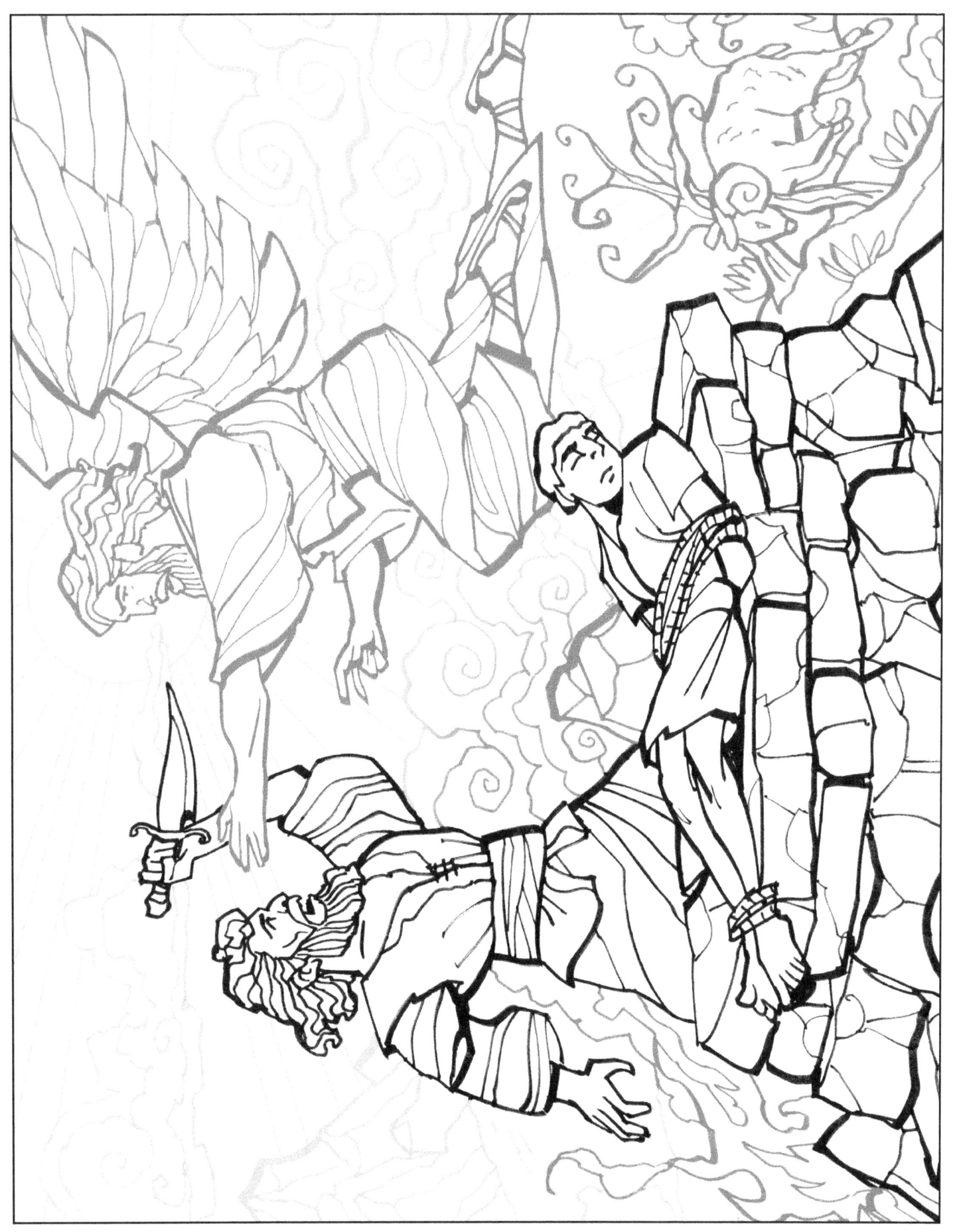

GOD PROVIDES THE SACRIFICE

Genesis 22:9

King James Bible

And they came to the place which God had told him of; and Abraham built an altar there, and laid the wood in order, and bound Isaac his son, and laid him on the altar upon the wood.

And Abraham stretched forth his hand, and took the knife to slay his son.

And the angel of the Lord called unto him out of heaven, and said, Abraham, Abraham: and he said, Here am I.

And he said, Lay not thine hand upon the lad, neither do thou any thing unto him: for now I know that thou fearest God, seeing thou hast not withheld thy son, thine only son from me.

And Abraham lifted up his eyes, and looked, and behold behind him a ram caught in a thicket by his horns: and Abraham went and took the ram, and offered him up for a burnt offering in the stead of his son.

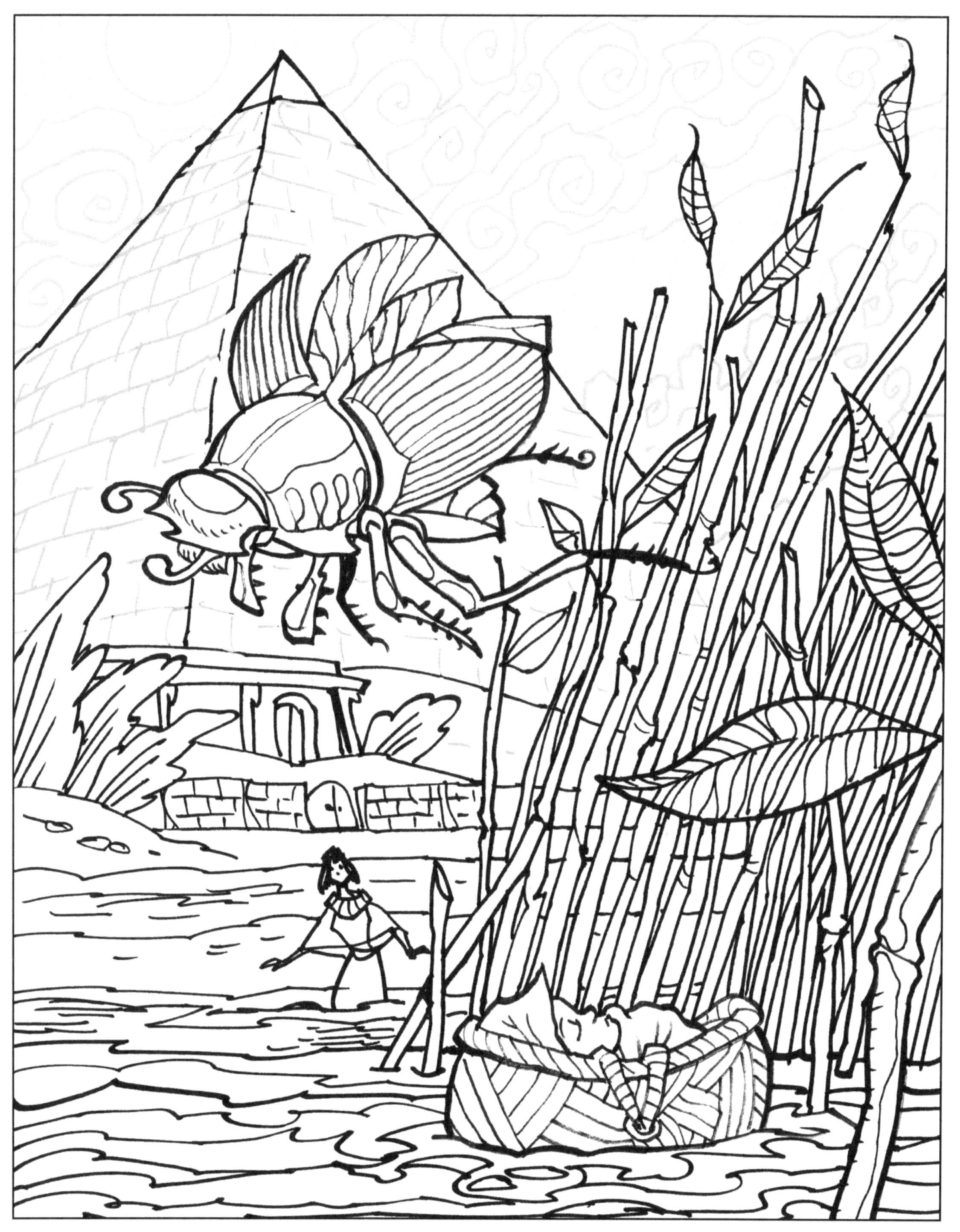

THE BABY IN THE BASKET

EXODUS 2:5
KING JAMES BIBLE

AND THE DAUGHTER OF PHARAOH CAME DOWN TO WASH HERSELF AT THE RIVER; AND HER MAIDENS WALKED ALONG BY THE RIVER'S SIDE; AND WHEN SHE SAW THE ARK AMONG THE FLAGS, SHE SENT HER MAID TO FETCH IT. AND WHEN SHE HAD OPENED IT, SHE SAW THE CHILD: AND, BEHOLD, THE BABE WEPT. AND SHE HAD COMPASSION ON HIM, AND SAID, THIS IS ONE OF THE HEBREWS' CHILDREN. THEN SAID HIS SISTER TO PHARAOH'S DAUGHTER, SHALL I GO AND CALL TO THEE A NURSE OF THE HEBREW WOMEN, THAT SHE MAY NURSE THE CHILD FOR THEE? AND PHARAOH'S DAUGHTER SAID TO HER, GO. AND THE MAID WENT AND CALLED THE CHILD'S MOTHER. AND PHARAOH'S DAUGHTER SAID UNTO HER, TAKE THIS CHILD AWAY, AND NURSE IT FOR ME, AND I WILL GIVE THEE THY WAGES. AND THE WOMAN TOOK THE CHILD, AND NURSED IT. 10AND THE CHILD GREW, AND SHE BROUGHT HIM UNTO PHARAOH'S DAUGHTER, AND HE BECAME HER SON. AND SHE CALLED HIS NAME MOSES: AND SHE SAID, BECAUSE I DREW HIM OUT OF THE WATER.

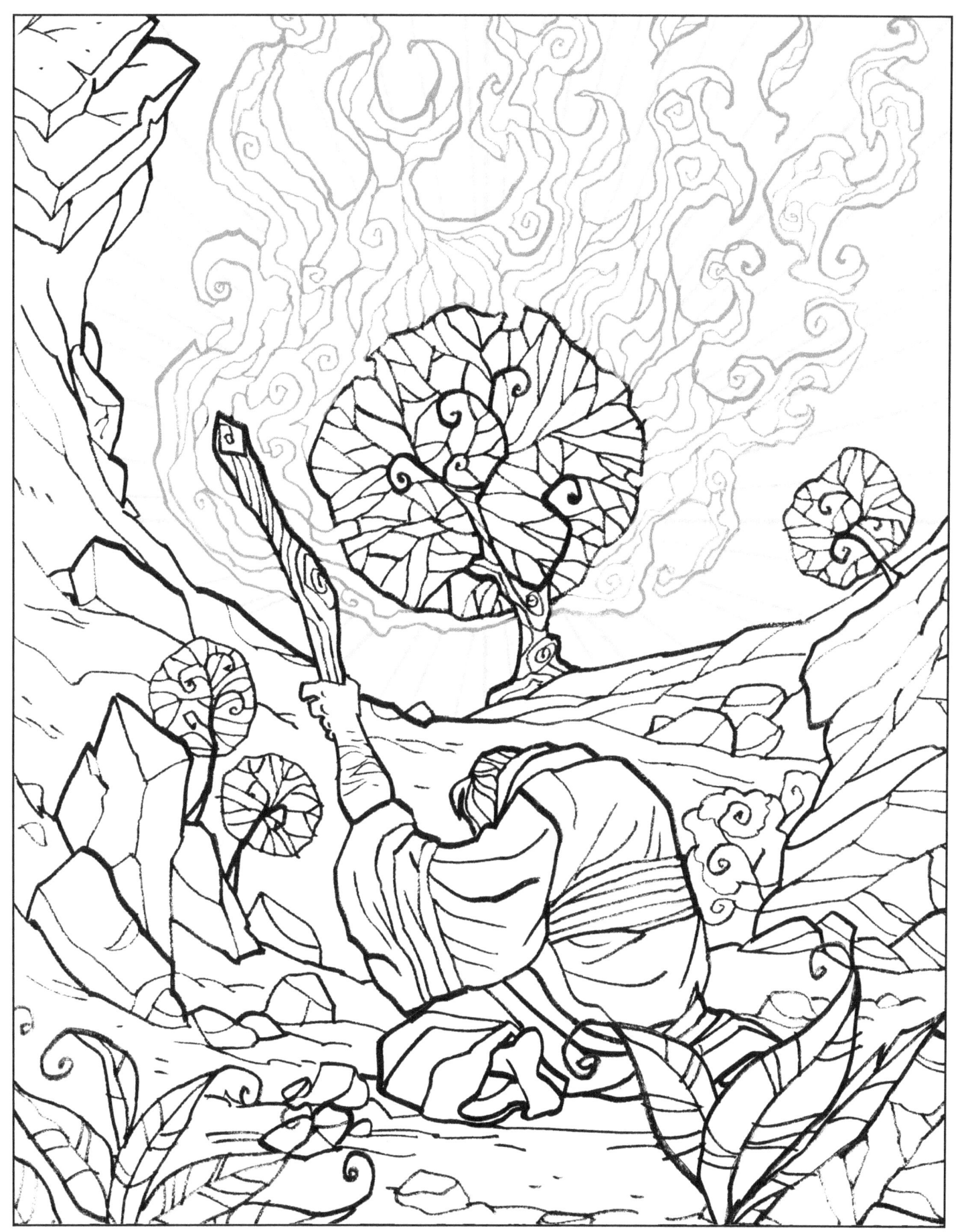

MOSES AND THE BURNING BUSH

Exodus 3:2
King James Bible

And the angel of the LORD appeared unto him in a flame of fire out of the midst of a bush: and he looked, and, behold, the bush burned with fire, and the bush was not consumed. And Moses said, I will now turn aside, and see this great sight, why the bush is not burnt. And when the LORD saw that he turned aside to see, God called unto him out of the midst of the bush, and said, Moses, Moses. And he said, Here am I. And he said, Draw not nigh hither: put off thy shoes from off thy feet, for the place whereon thou standest is holy ground.

Exodus 3:10
King James Bible

Come now therefore, and I will send thee unto Pharaoh, that thou mayest bring forth my people the children of Israel out of Egypt.

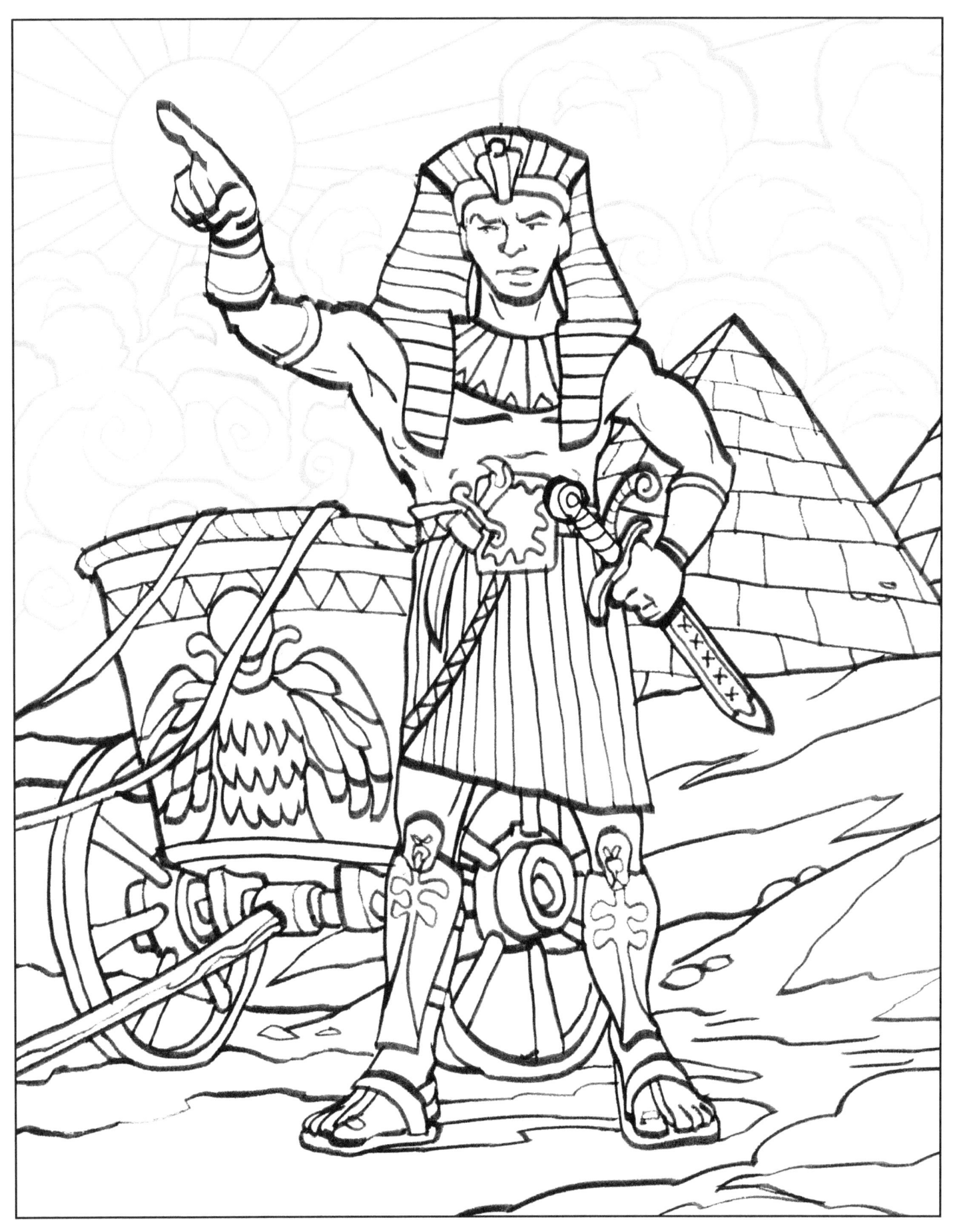

Pharaoh will not let the People Go

Exodus 14:5
King James Bible

And it was told the king of Egypt that the people fled: and the heart of Pharaoh and of his servants was turned against the people, and they said, Why have we done this, that we have let Israel go from serving us? And he made ready his chariot, and took his people with him: And he took six hundred chosen chariots, and all the chariots of Egypt, and captains over every one of them. And the LORD hardened the heart of Pharaoh king of Egypt, and he pursued after the children of Israel: and the children of Israel went out with an high hand. But the Egyptians pursued after them, all the horses and chariots of Pharaoh, and his horsemen, and his army, and overtook them encamping by the sea, beside Pihahiroth, before Baalzephon.

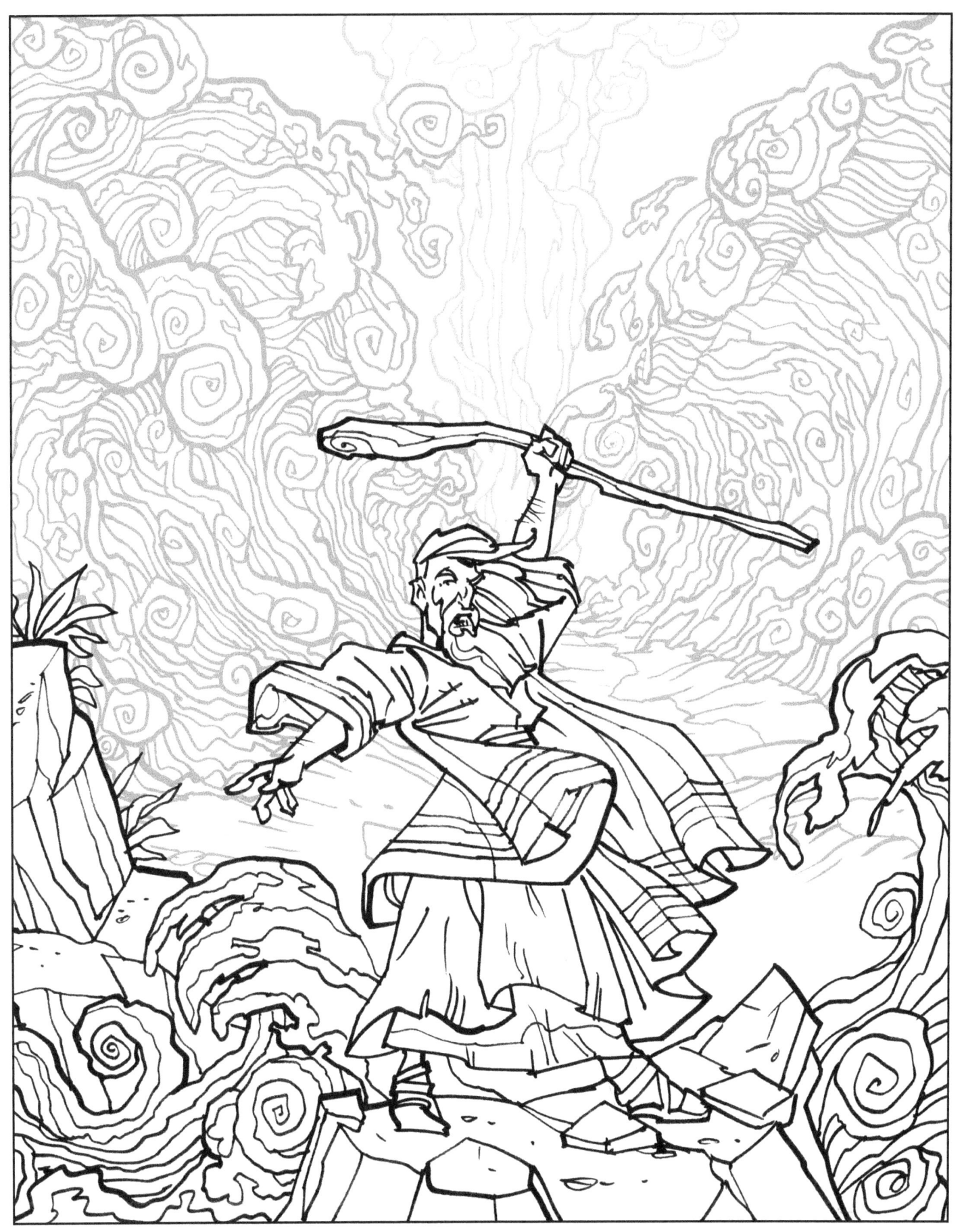

The Parting of the Sea

Exodus 14:21
King James Bible

And Moses stretched out his hand over the sea; and the LORD caused the sea to go back by a strong east wind all that night, and made the sea dry land, and the waters were divided. And the children of Israel went into the midst of the sea upon the dry ground: and the waters were a wall unto them on their right hand, and on their left. And the Egyptians pursued, and went in after them to the midst of the sea, even all Pharaoh's horses, his chariots, and his horsemen. And it came to pass, that in the morning watch the LORD looked unto the host of the Egyptians through the pillar of fire and of the cloud, and troubled the host of the Egyptians, And took off their chariot wheels, that they drave them heavily: so that the Egyptians said, Let us flee from the face of Israel; for the LORD fighteth for them against the Egyptians.

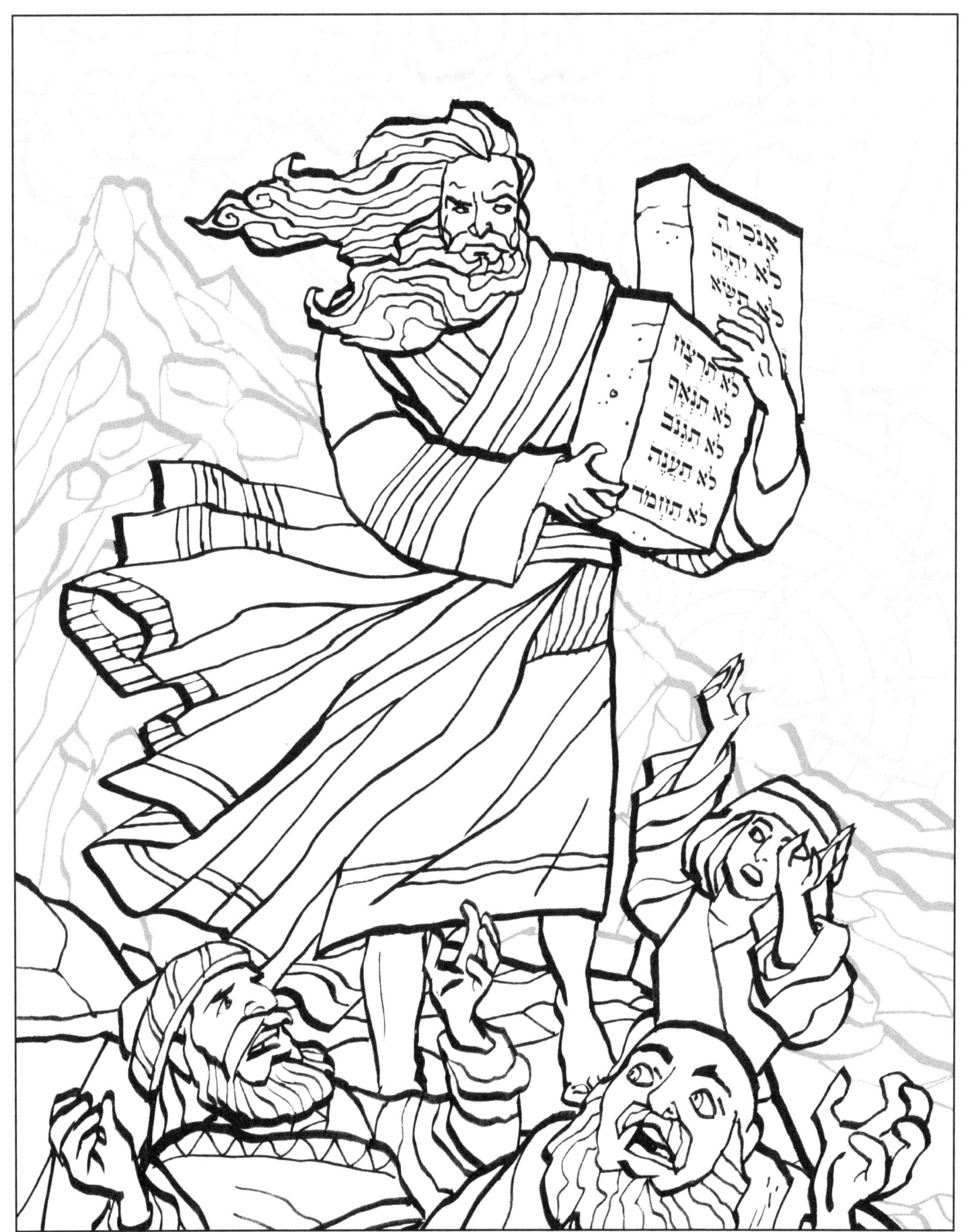

AND GOD SPOKE

Exodus 19:23-25

King James Bible

And Moses said unto the Lord, The people cannot come up to mount Sinai: for thou chargedst us, saying, Set bounds about the mount, and sanctify it.
And the Lord said unto him, Away, get thee down, and thou shalt come up, thou, and Aaron with thee: but let not the priests and the people break through to come up unto the Lord, lest he break forth upon them.
So Moses went down unto the people, and spake unto them.

Exodus 20:1-5

And God spake all these words, saying,
I am the Lord thy God, which have brought thee out of the land of Egypt, out of the house of bondage.
Thou shalt have no other gods before me.
Thou shalt not make unto thee any graven image, or any likeness of any thing that is in heaven above, or that is in the earth beneath, or that is in the water under the earth.
Thou shalt not bow down thyself to them, nor serve them: for I the Lord thy God am a jealous God,

Exodus 20:7-8

Thou shalt not take the name of the Lord thy God in vain; for the Lord will not hold him guiltless that taketh his name in vain.
Remember the sabbath day, to keep it holy.
Honour thy father and thy mother: that thy days may be long upon the land which the Lord thy God giveth thee.

Exodus 20:13-8

Thou shalt not kill.
Thou shalt not commit adultery.
Thou shalt not steal.
Thou shalt not bear false witness against thy neighbour.
Thou shalt not covet thy neighbour's house, thou shalt not covet thy neighbour's wife, nor his manservant, nor his maidservant, nor his ox, nor his ass, nor any thing that is thy neighbour's.

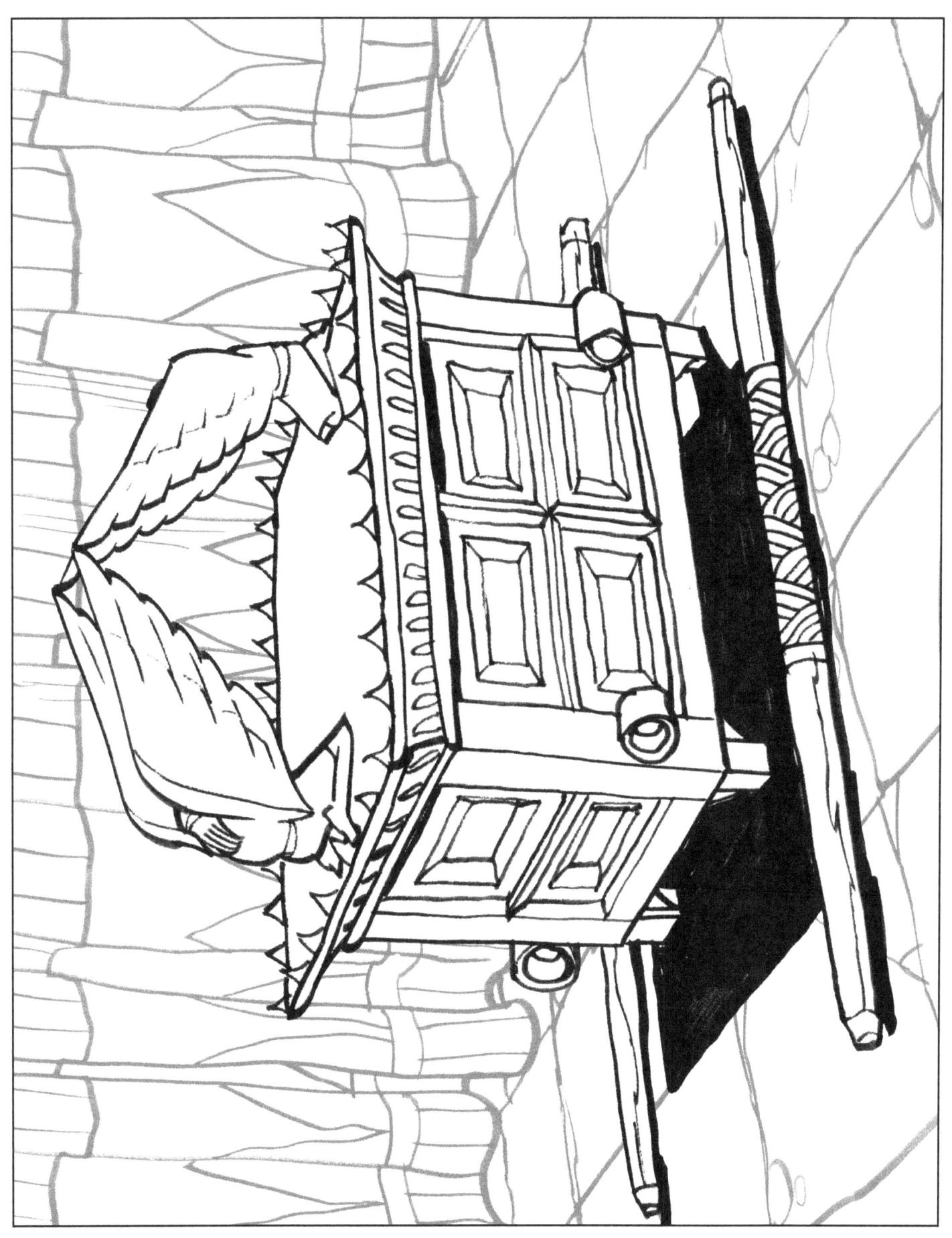

THE ARK OR THE LORD

Exodus 37:1
King James Bible

And Bezaleel made the ark of shittim wood: two cubits and a half was the length of it, and a cubit and a half the breadth of it, and a cubit and a half the height of it:

And he overlaid it with pure gold within and without, and made a crown of gold to it round about.

And he cast for it four rings of gold, to be set by the four corners of it; even two rings upon the one side of it, and two rings upon the other side of it.

And he made staves of shittim wood, and overlaid them with gold.

And he put the staves into the rings by the sides of the ark, to bear the ark.

And he made the mercy seat of pure gold: two cubits and a half was the length thereof, and one cubit and a half the breadth thereof.

And he made two cherubims of gold, beaten out of one piece made he them, on the two ends of the mercy seat;

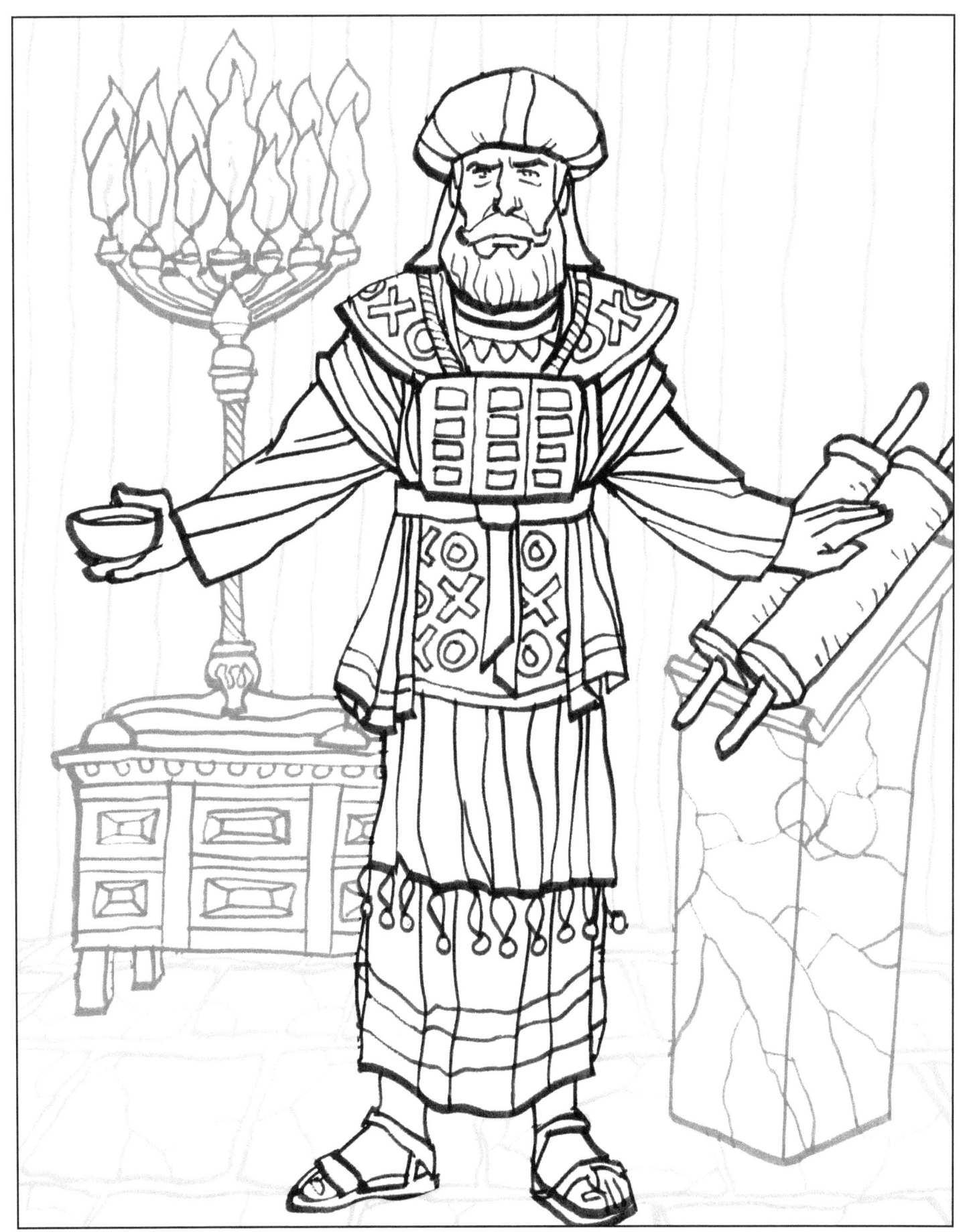

SERVICE OF THE TABERNACLE

NUMBERS 18:6
KING JAMES BIBLE

AND I, BEHOLD, I HAVE TAKEN YOUR BRETHREN THE LEVITES FROM AMONG THE CHILDREN OF ISRAEL: TO YOU THEY ARE GIVEN AS A GIFT FOR THE LORD, TO DO THE SERVICE OF THE TABERNACLE OF THE CONGREGATION.

THEREFORE THOU AND THY SONS WITH THEE SHALL KEEP YOUR PRIEST'S OFFICE FOR EVERY THING OF THE ALTAR, AND WITHIN THE VAIL; AND YE SHALL SERVE: I HAVE GIVEN YOUR PRIEST'S OFFICE UNTO YOU AS A SERVICE OF GIFT: AND THE STRANGER THAT COMETH NIGH SHALL BE PUT TO DEATH.

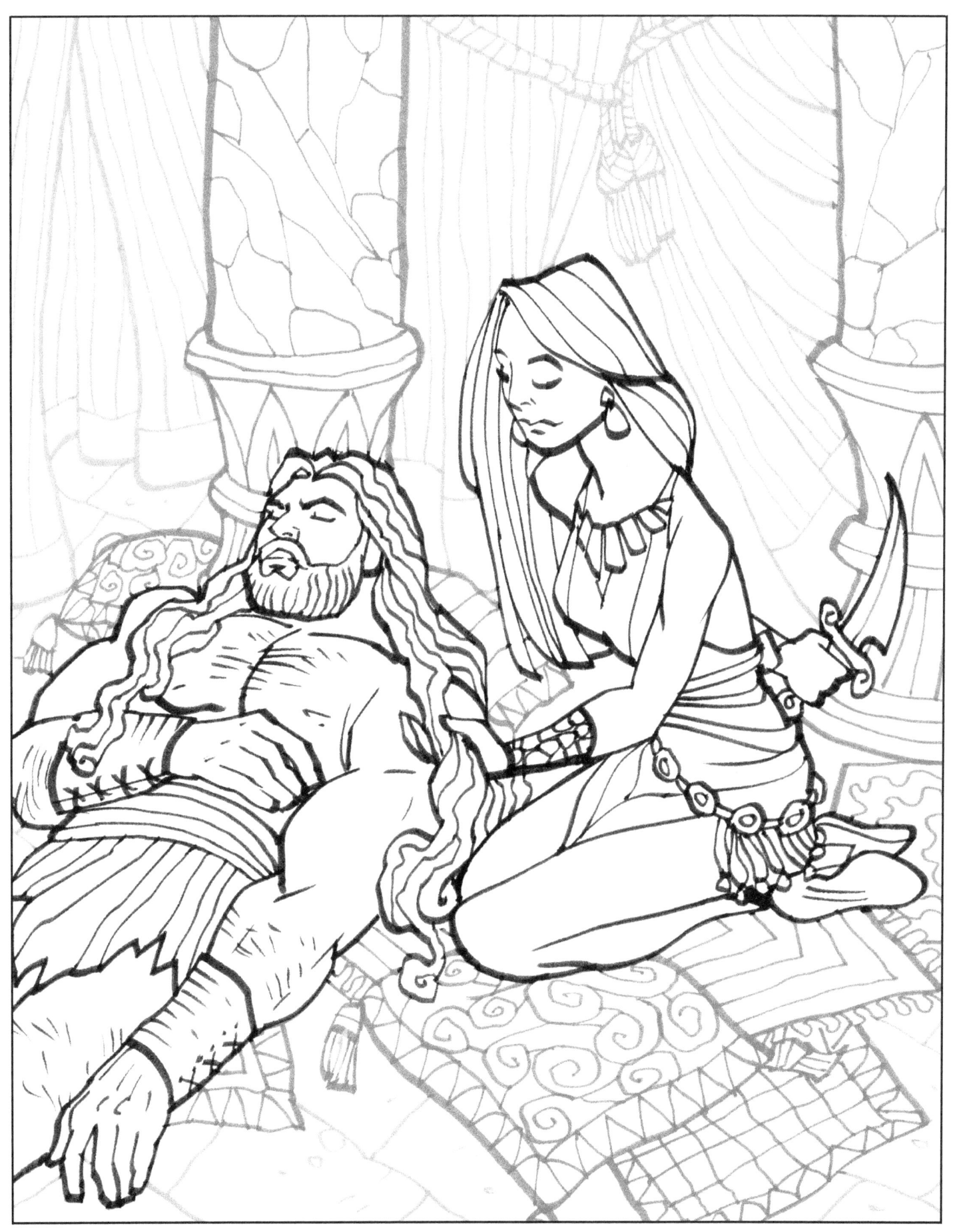

SAMSON AND DELILAH

Judges 16:16
King James Bible

And it came to pass, when she pressed him daily with her words, and urged him, so that his soul was vexed unto death;

That he told her all his heart, and said unto her, There hath not come a razor upon mine head; for I have been a Nazarite unto God from my mother's womb: if I be shaven, then my strength will go from me, and I shall become weak, and be like any other man.

And when Delilah saw that he had told her all his heart, she sent and called for the lords of the Philistines, saying, Come up this once, for he hath shewed me all his heart. Then the lords of the Philistines came up unto her, and brought money in their hand.

And she made him sleep upon her knees; and she called for a man, and she caused him to shave off the seven locks of his head; and she began to afflict him, and his strength went from him.

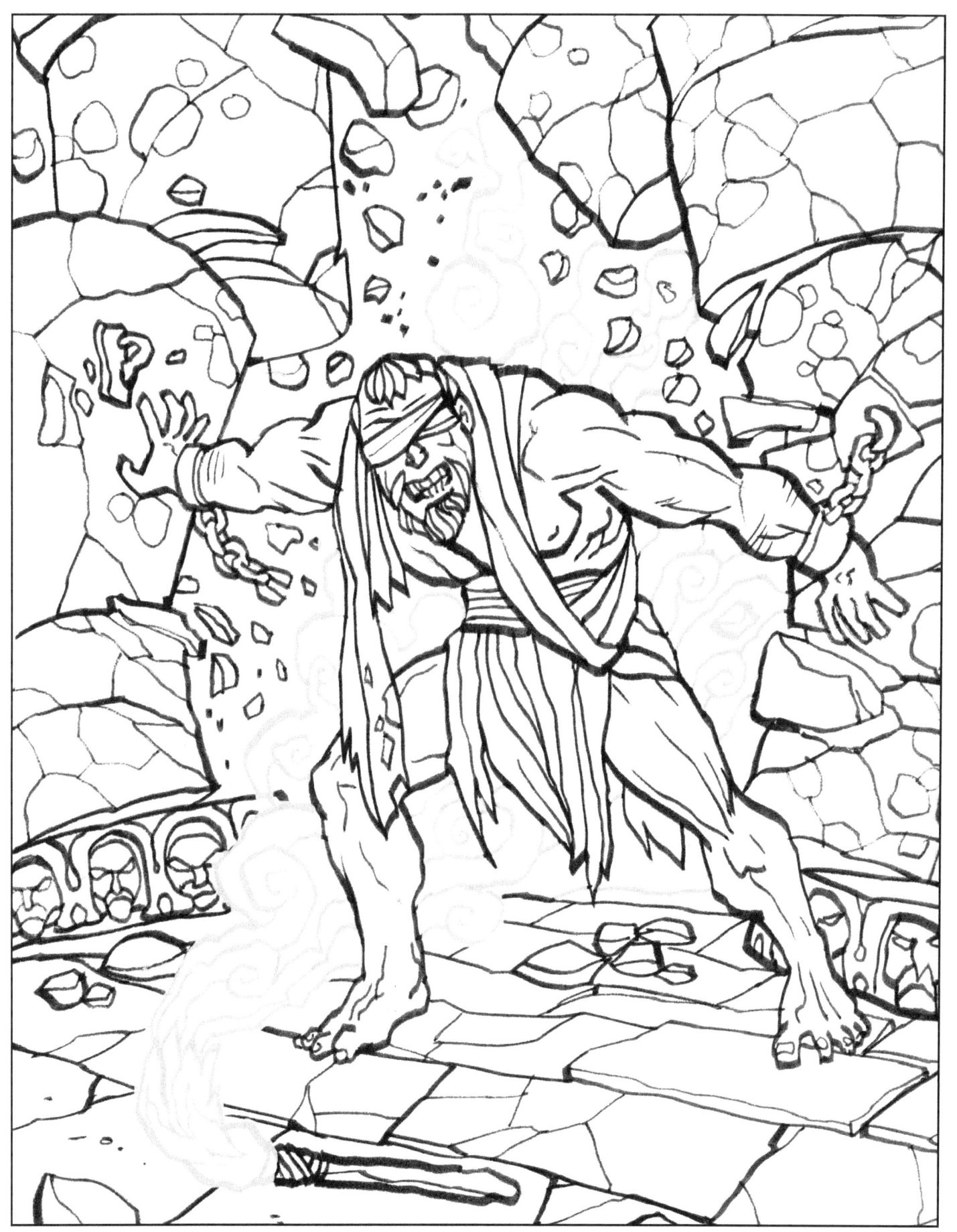

SAMSON CALLS UPON THE LORD

Judges 16:28

King James Bible

And Samson called unto the Lord, and said, O Lord God, remember me, I pray thee, and strengthen me, I pray thee, only this once, O God, that I may be at once avenged of the Philistines for my two eyes.

And Samson took hold of the two middle pillars upon which the house stood, and on which it was borne up, of the one with his right hand, and of the other with his left.

And Samson said, Let me die with the Philistines. And he bowed himself with all his might; and the house fell upon the lords, and upon all the people that were therein. So the dead which he slew at his death were more than they which he slew in his life.

Then his brethren and all the house of his father came down, and took him, and brought him up, and buried him between Zorah and Eshtaol in the buryingplace of Manoah his father. And he judged Israel twenty years.

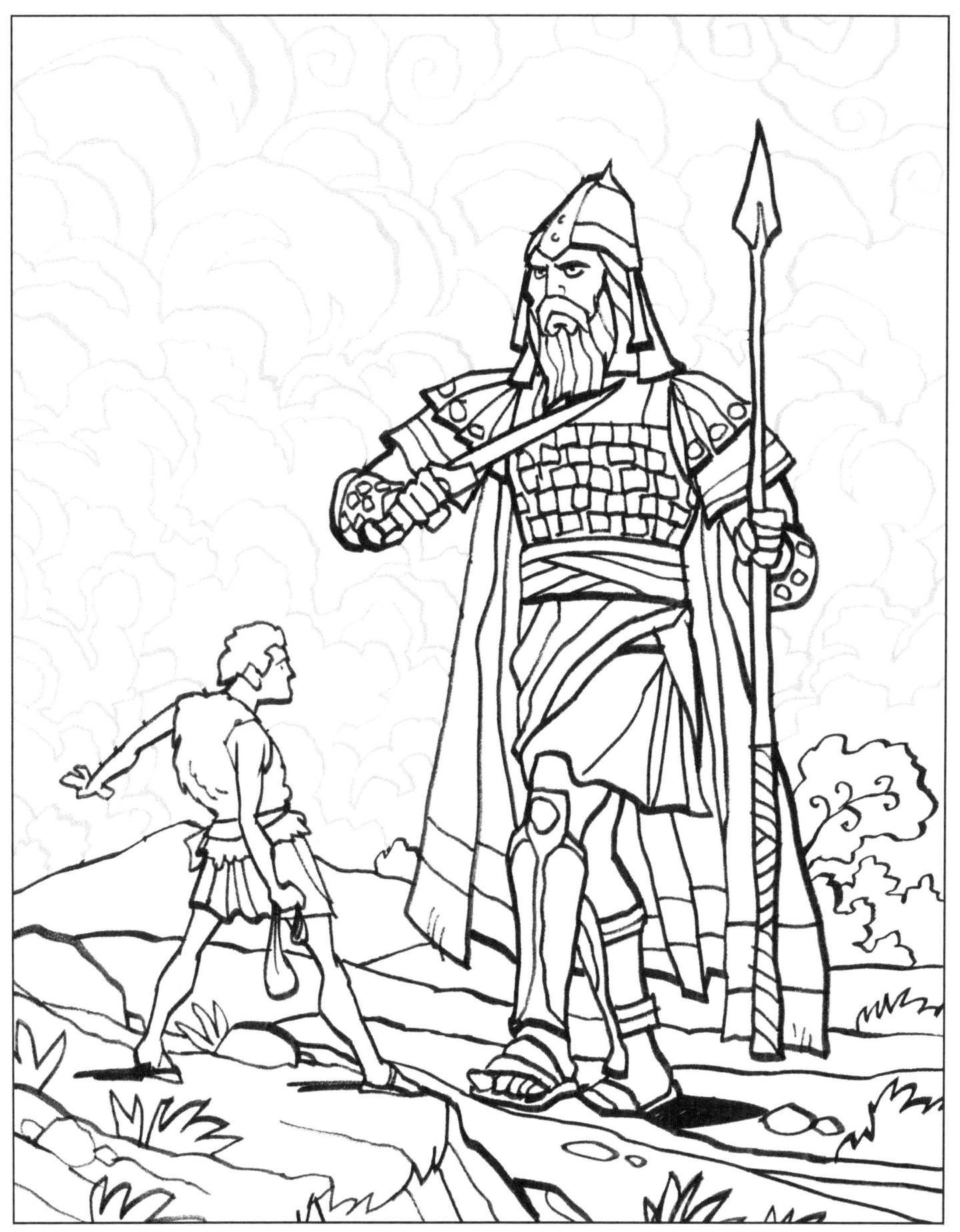

DAVID AND GOLIATH

1 Samuel 17:4
King James Bible

And there went out a champion out of the camp of the Philistines, named Goliath, of Gath, whose height was six cubits and a span.

And he had an helmet of brass upon his head, and he was armed with a coat of mail; and the weight of the coat was five thousand shekels of brass.

And he had greaves of brass upon his legs, and a target of brass between his shoulders.

And the staff of his spear was like a weaver's beam; and his spear's head weighed six hundred shekels of iron: and one bearing a shield went before him.

And he stood and cried unto the armies of Israel, and said unto them, Why are ye come out to set your battle in array? am not I a Philistine, and ye servants to Saul? choose you a man for you, and let him come down to me.

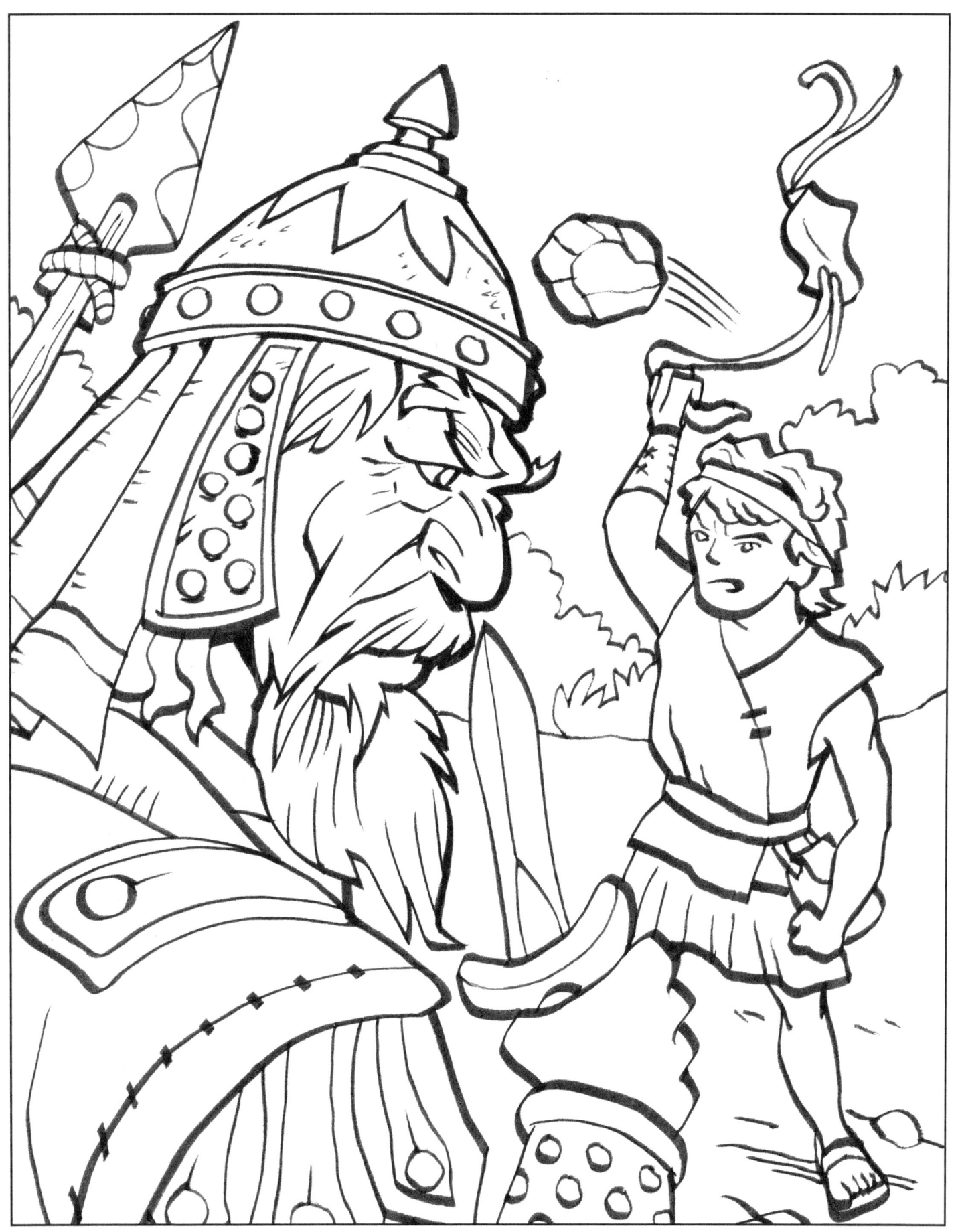

DAVID BEATS HIS ENEMY

1 Samuel 17:42

King James Bible

And when the Philistine looked about, and saw David, he disdained him: for he was but a youth, and ruddy, and of a fair countenance.

And the Philistine said unto David, Am I a dog, that thou comest to me with staves? And the Philistine cursed David by his gods.

And the Philistine said to David, Come to me, and I will give thy flesh unto the fowls of the air, and to the beasts of the field.

Then said David to the Philistine, Thou comest to me with a sword, and with a spear, and with a shield: but I come to thee in the name of the Lord of hosts, the God of the armies of Israel, whom thou hast defied.

This day will the Lord deliver thee into mine hand; and I will smite thee, and take thine head from thee; and I will give the carcases of the host of the Philistines this day unto the fowls of the air, and to the wild beasts of the earth; that all the earth may know that there is a God in Israel.

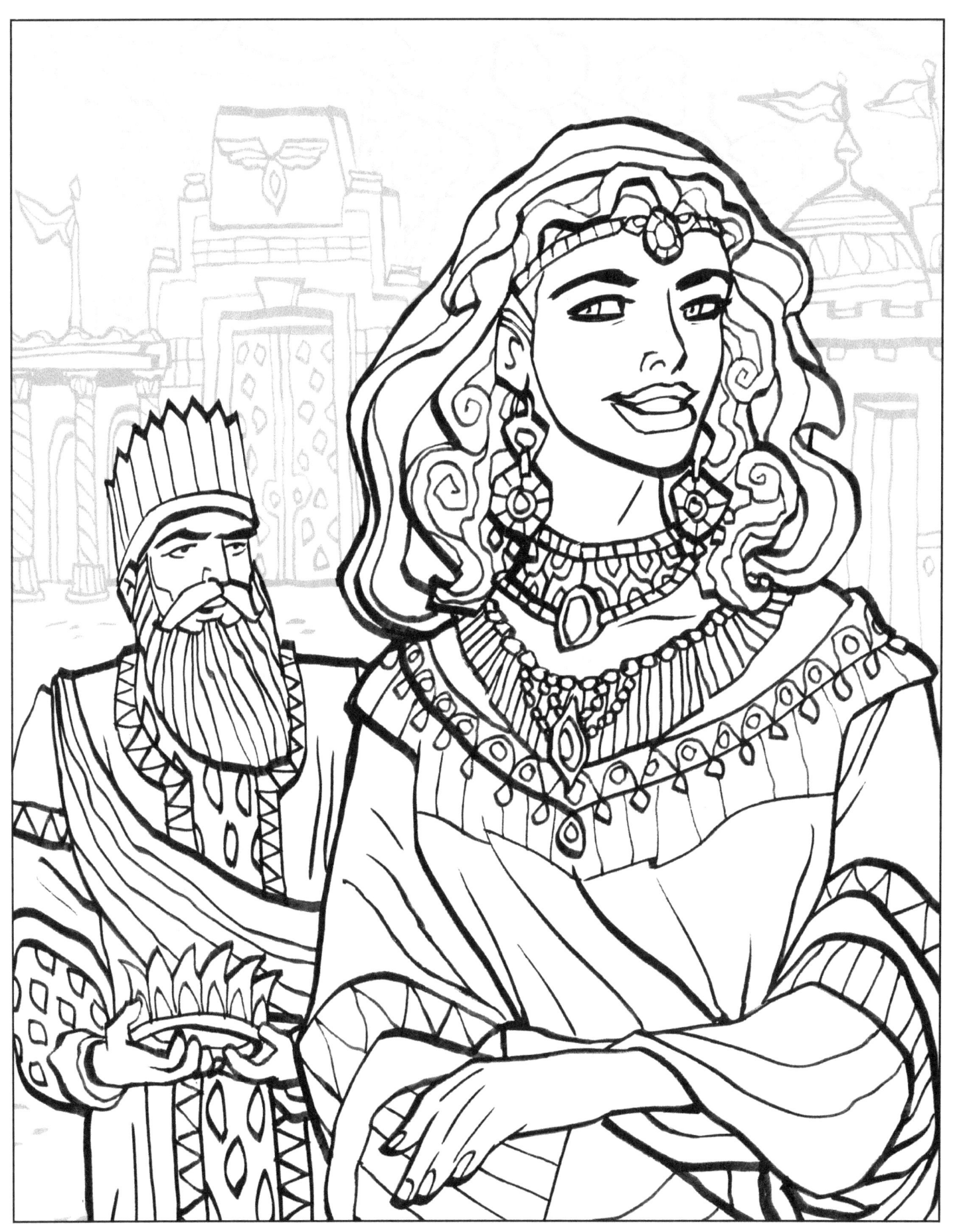

AND THE KING LOVED ESTHER ABOVE ALL

Esther 2 :16
King James Bible

So Esther was taken unto king Ahasuerus into his house royal in the tenth month, which is the month Tebeth, in the seventh year of his reign.

And the king loved Esther above all the women, and she obtained grace and favour in his sight more than all the virgins; so that he set the royal crown upon her head, and made her queen instead of Vashti.

Then the king made a great feast unto all his princes and his servants, even Esther's feast; and he made a release to the provinces, and gave gifts, according to the state of the king.

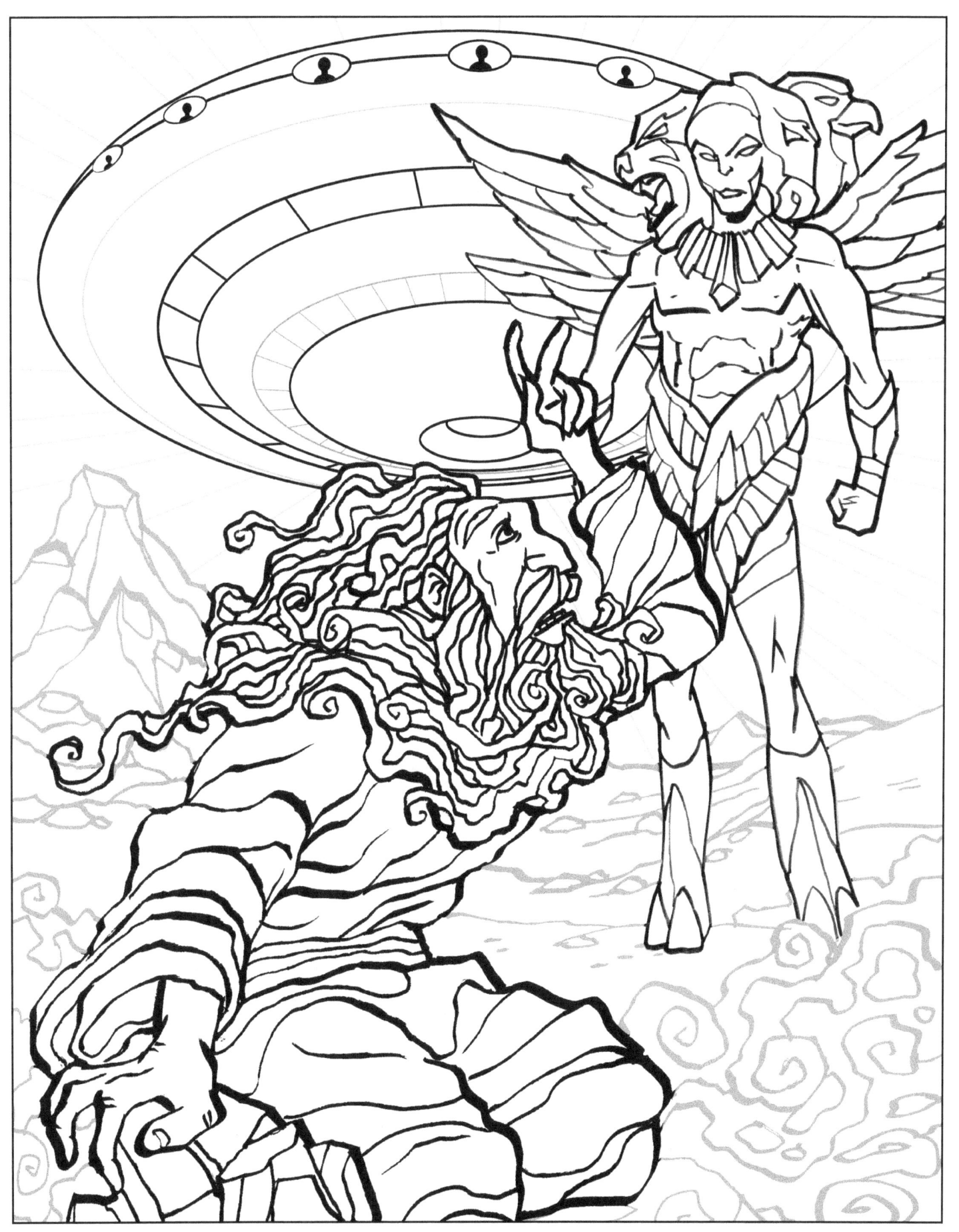

A Wheel in the middle of A Wheel

Ezekiel 1:1
King James Bible

As for the likeness of the living creatures, their appearance was like burning coals of fire, and like the appearance of lamps: it went up and down among the living creatures; and the fire was bright, and out of the fire went forth lightning.

And the living creatures ran and returned as the appearance of a flash of lightning.

Now as I beheld the living creatures, behold one wheel upon the earth by the living creatures, with his four faces.

The appearance of the wheels and their work was like unto the colour of a beryl: and they four had one likeness: and their appearance and their work was as it were a wheel in the middle of a wheel.

When they went, they went upon their four sides: and they turned not when they went.

As for their rings, they were so high that they were dreadful; and their rings were full of eyes round about them four.

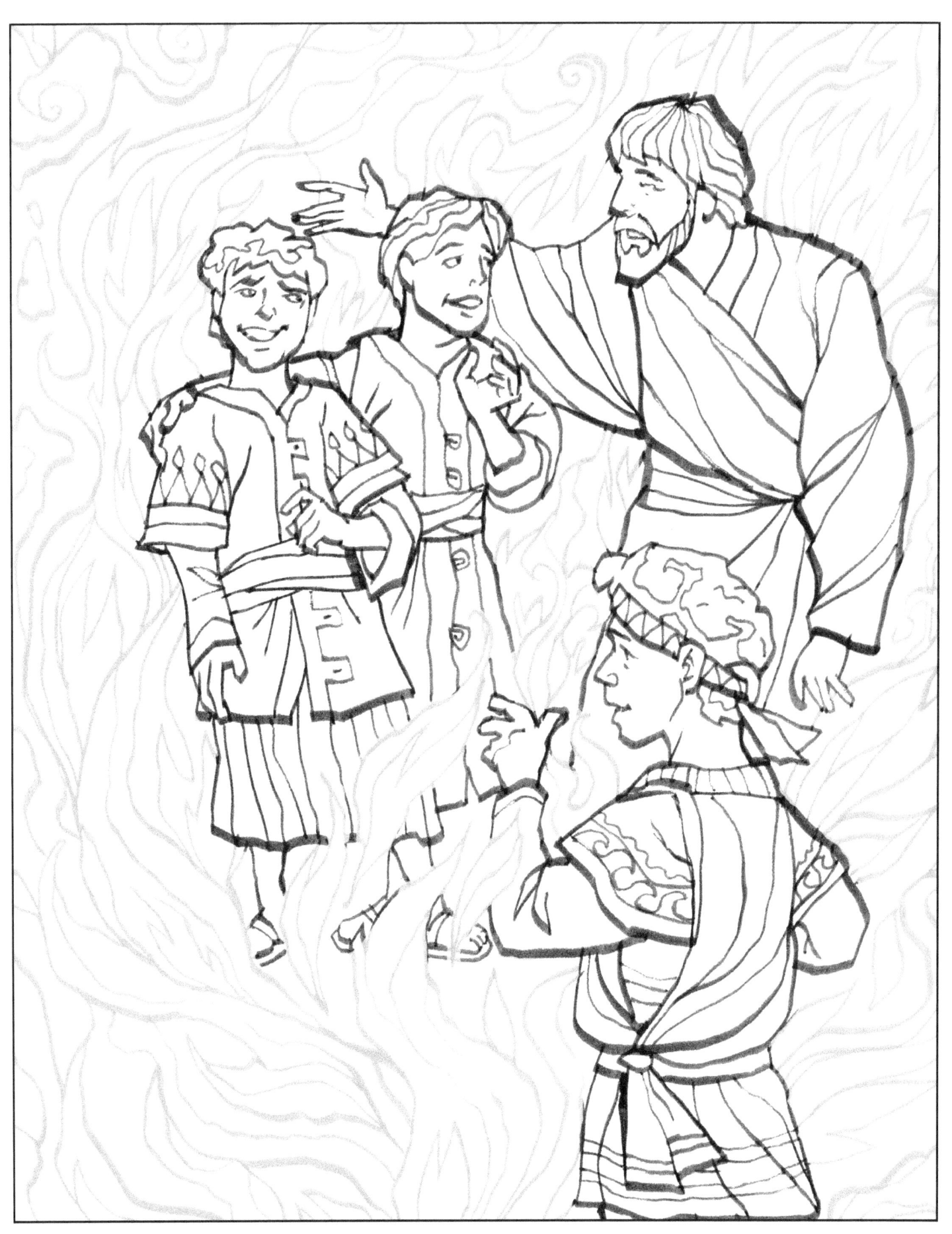

THE FOURTH IS LIKE THE SON OF GOD

Daniel 3 :23
King James Bible

And these three men, Shadrach, Meshach, and Abednego, fell down bound into the midst of the burning fiery furnace.

Then Nebuchadnezzar the king was astonished, and rose up in haste, and spake, and said unto his counsellors, Did not we cast three men bound into the midst of the fire? They answered and said unto the king, True, O king.

He answered and said, Lo, I see four men loose, walking in the midst of the fire, and they have no hurt; and the form of the fourth is like the Son of God.

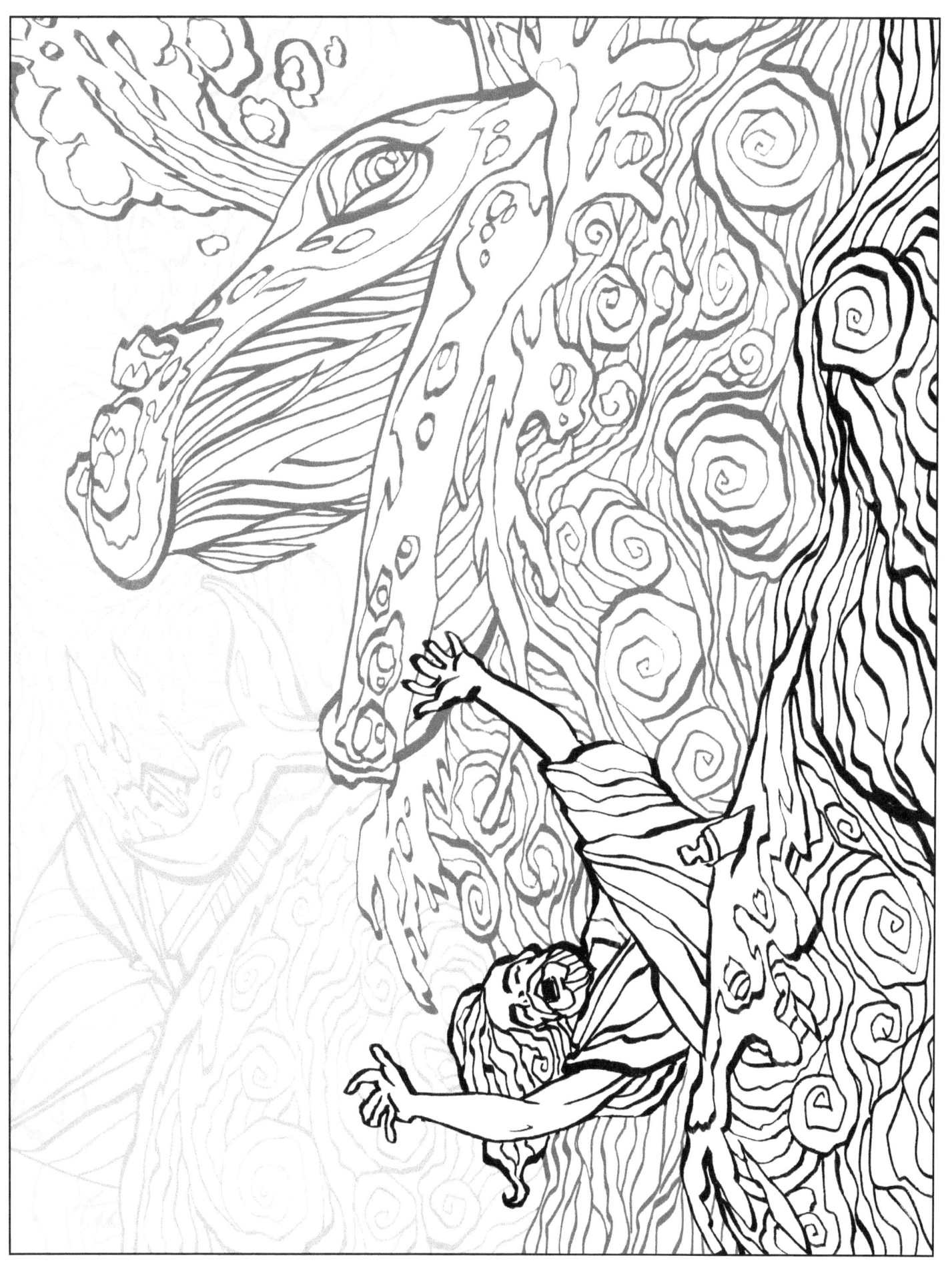

A Great Fish Swallowed Up Jonah

JONAH 1 :11
KING JAMES BIBLE

WHEREFORE THEY CRIED UNTO THE LORD, AND SAID, WE BESEECH THEE, O LORD, WE BESEECH THEE, LET US NOT PERISH FOR THIS MAN'S LIFE, AND LAY NOT UPON US INNOCENT BLOOD: FOR THOU, O LORD, HAST DONE AS IT PLEASED THEE.

SO THEY TOOK UP JONAH, AND CAST HIM FORTH INTO THE SEA: AND THE SEA CEASED FROM HER RAGING.

THEN THE MEN FEARED THE LORD EXCEEDINGLY, AND OFFERED A SACRIFICE UNTO THE LORD, AND MADE VOWS.

NOW THE LORD HAD PREPARED A GREAT FISH TO SWALLOW UP JONAH. AND JONAH WAS IN THE BELLY OF THE FISH THREE DAYS AND THREE NIGHTS.

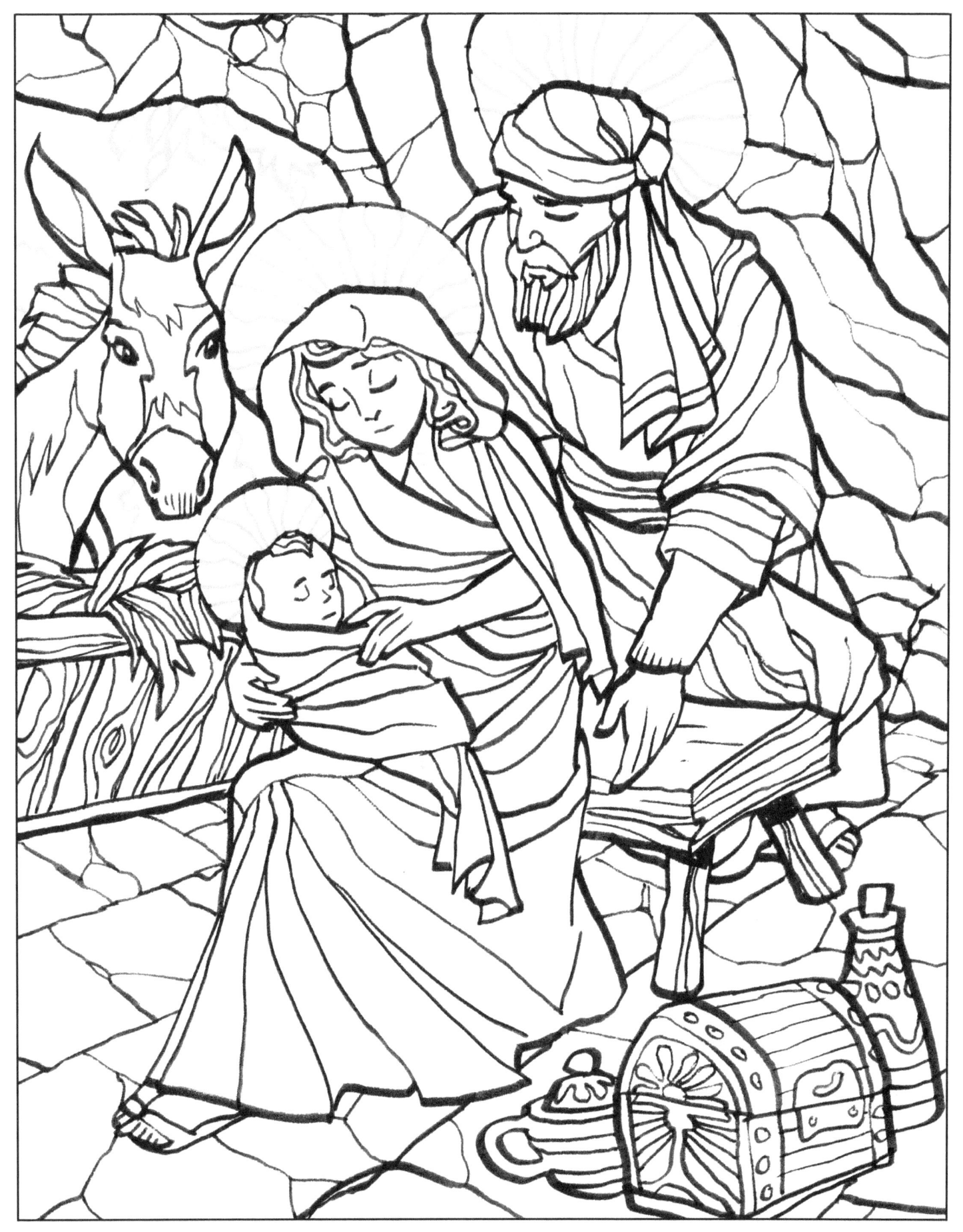

BEHOLD A VIRGIN SHALL BE WITH CHILD

Matthew 1:21
King James Bible

And she shall bring forth a son, and thou shalt call his name Jesus: for he shall save his people from their sins.

Now all this was done, that it might be fulfilled which was spoken of the Lord by the prophet, saying,

Behold, a virgin shall be with child, and shall bring forth a son, and they shall call his name Emmanuel, which being interpreted is, God with us.

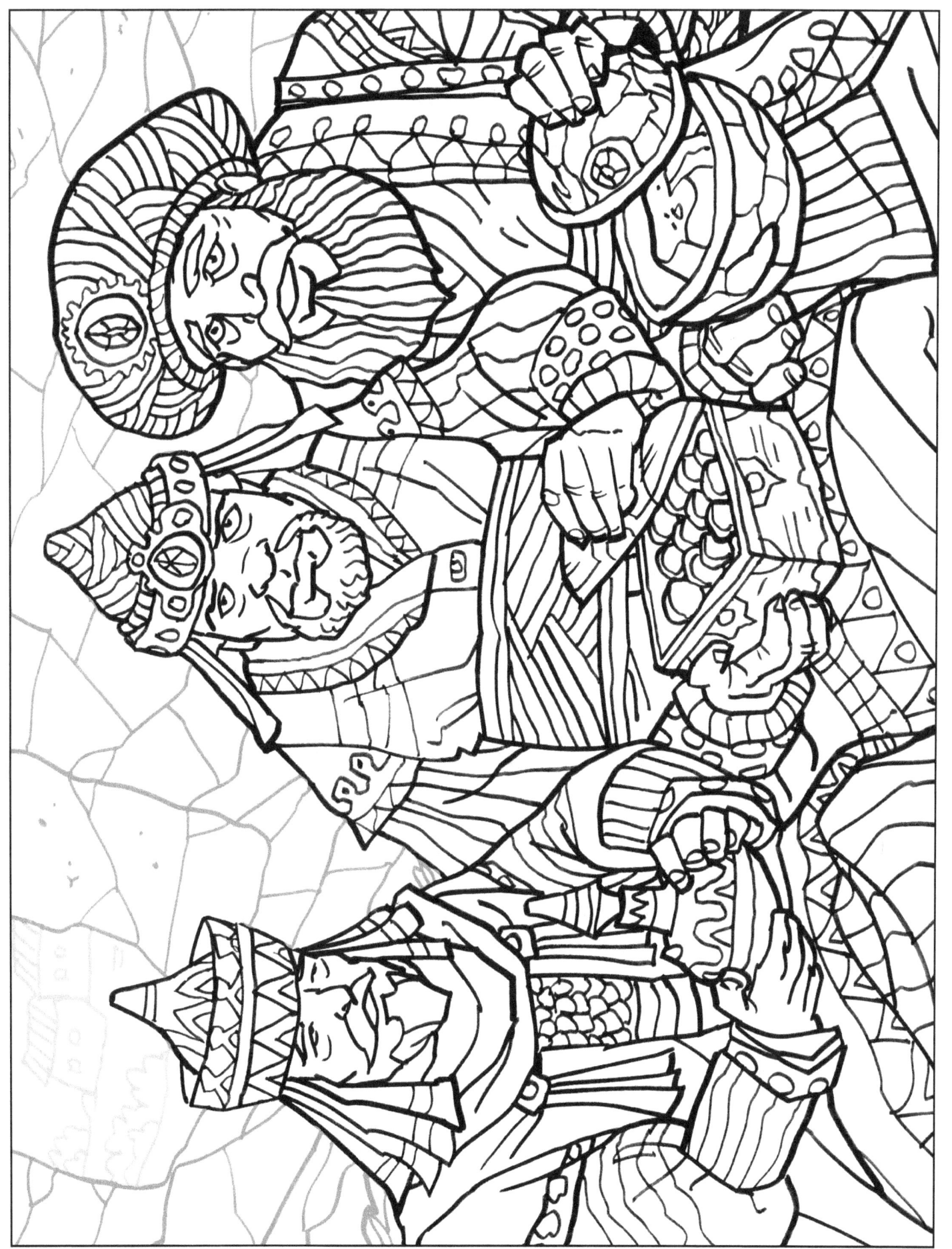

Three Wise Men

Matthew 2 :1
King James Bible

Now when Jesus was born in Bethlehem of Judaea in the days of Herod the king, behold, there came wise men from the east to Jerusalem,

Saying, Where is he that is born King of the Jews? for we have seen his star in the east, and are come to worship him.

When Herod the king had heard these things, he was troubled, and all Jerusalem with him.

And when he had gathered all the chief priests and scribes of the people together, he demanded of them where Christ should be born.

And they said unto him, In Bethlehem of Judaea: for thus it is written by the prophet,

And thou Bethlehem, in the land of Juda, art not the least among the princes of Juda: for out of thee shall come a Governor, that shall rule my people Israel.

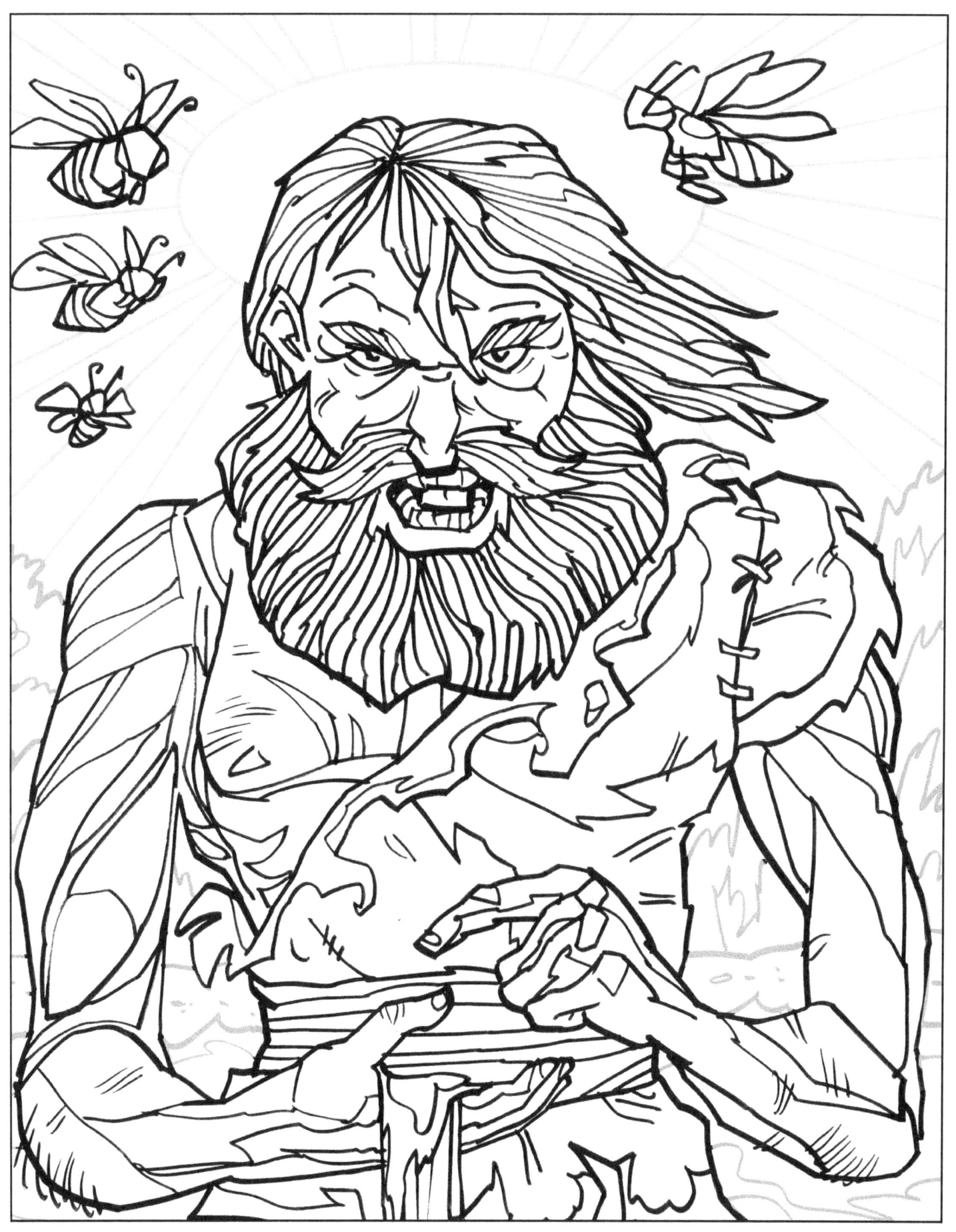

JOHN THE BAPTIST

Matthew 3 :1
King James Bible

In those days came John the Baptist, preaching in the wilderness of Judaea,

And saying, Repent ye: for the kingdom of heaven is at hand.

For this is he that was spoken of by the prophet Esaias, saying, The voice of one crying in the wilderness, Prepare ye the way of the Lord, make his paths straight.

And the same John had his raiment of camel's hair, and a leathern girdle about his loins; and his meat was locusts and wild honey.

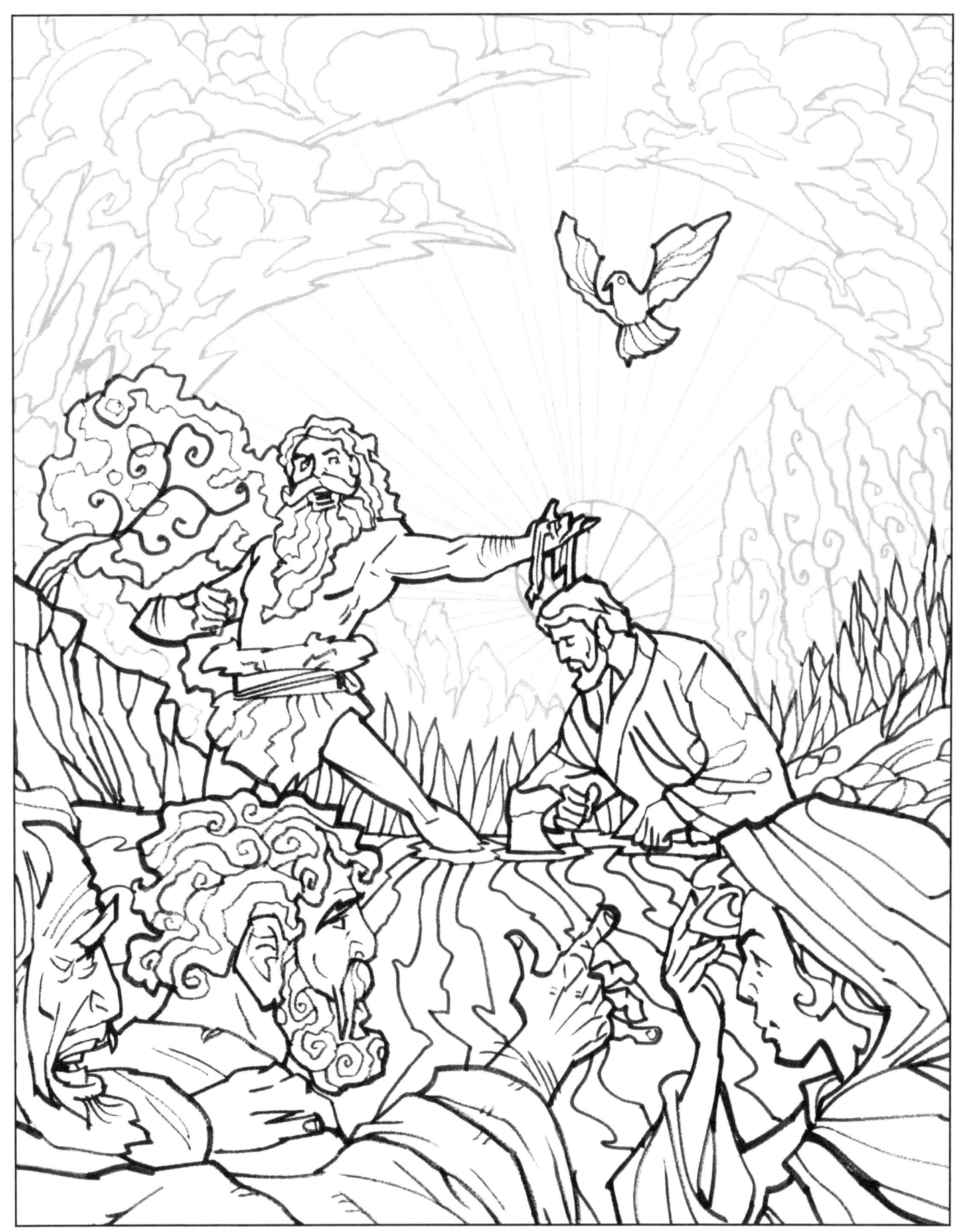

THIS IS MY BELOVED SON

Matthew 3 :11

King James Bible

I indeed baptize you with water unto repentance. But he that cometh after me is mightier than I, whose shoes I am not worthy to bear: he shall baptize you with the Holy Ghost, and with fire:

Whose fan is in his hand, and he will throughly purge his floor, and gather his wheat into the garner; but he will burn up the chaff with unquenchable fire.

Then cometh Jesus from Galilee to Jordan unto John, to be baptized of him.

But John forbad him, saying, I have need to be baptized of thee, and comest thou to me?

And Jesus answering said unto him, Suffer it to be so now: for thus it becometh us to fulfil all righteousness. Then he suffered him.

And Jesus, when he was baptized, went up straightway out of the water: and, lo, the heavens were opened unto him, and he saw the Spirit of God descending like a dove, and lighting upon him: And lo a voice from heaven, saying, This is my beloved Son, in whom I am well pleased.

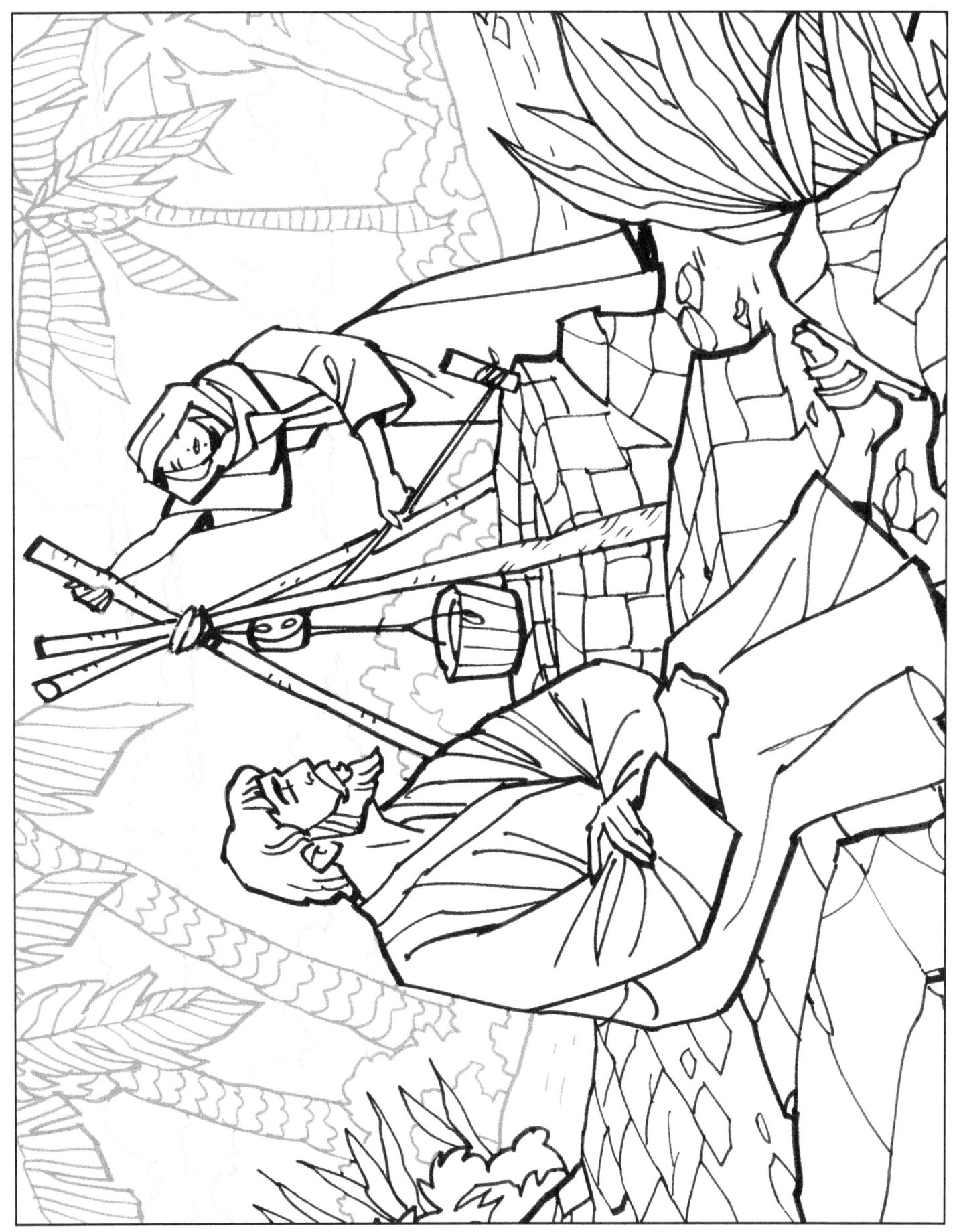

THE WOMAN AT THE WELL

John 4:9

King James Bible

Then saith the woman of Samaria unto him, How is it that thou, being a Jew, askest drink of me, which am a woman of Samaria? for the Jews have no dealings with the Samaritans.

Jesus answered and said unto her, If thou knewest the gift of God, and who it is that saith to thee, Give me to drink; thou wouldest have asked of him, and he would have given thee living water.

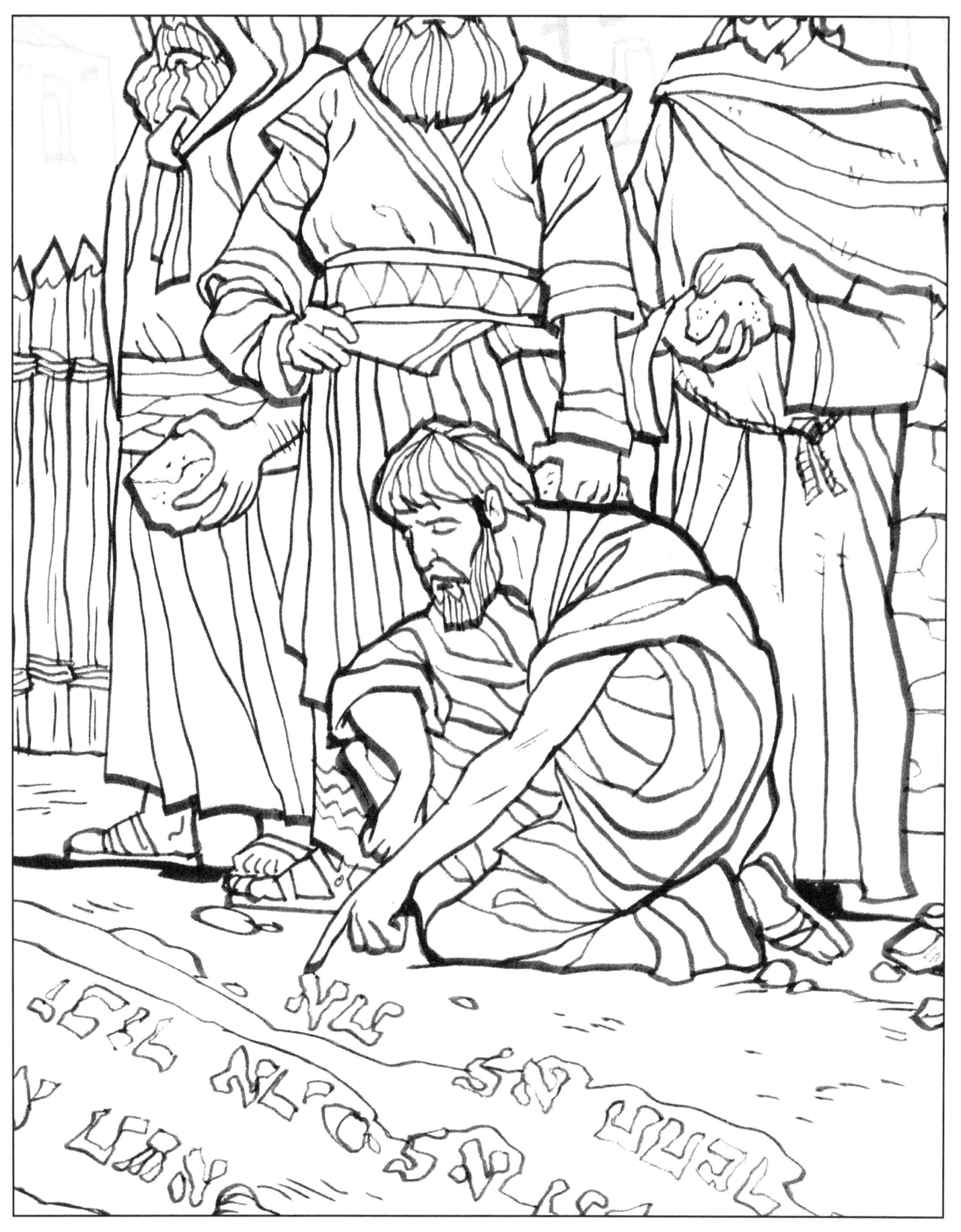

He Who Is Without Sin Cast The First Stone

John 8:4
King James Bible

They say unto him, Master, this woman was taken in adultery, in the very act. Now Moses in the law commanded us, that such should be stoned: but what sayest thou?

This they said, tempting him, that they might have to accuse him. But Jesus stooped down, and with his finger wrote on the ground, as though he heard them not.

So when they continued asking him, he lifted up himself, and said unto them, He that is without sin among you, let him first cast a stone at her. And again he stooped down, and wrote on the ground.

And they which heard it, being convicted by their own conscience, went out one by one, beginning at the eldest, even unto the last: and Jesus was left alone, and the woman standing in the midst.

When Jesus had lifted up himself, and saw none but the woman, he said unto her, Woman, where are those thine accusers? hath no man condemned thee?

She said, No man, Lord. And Jesus said unto her, Neither do I condemn thee: go, and sin no more.

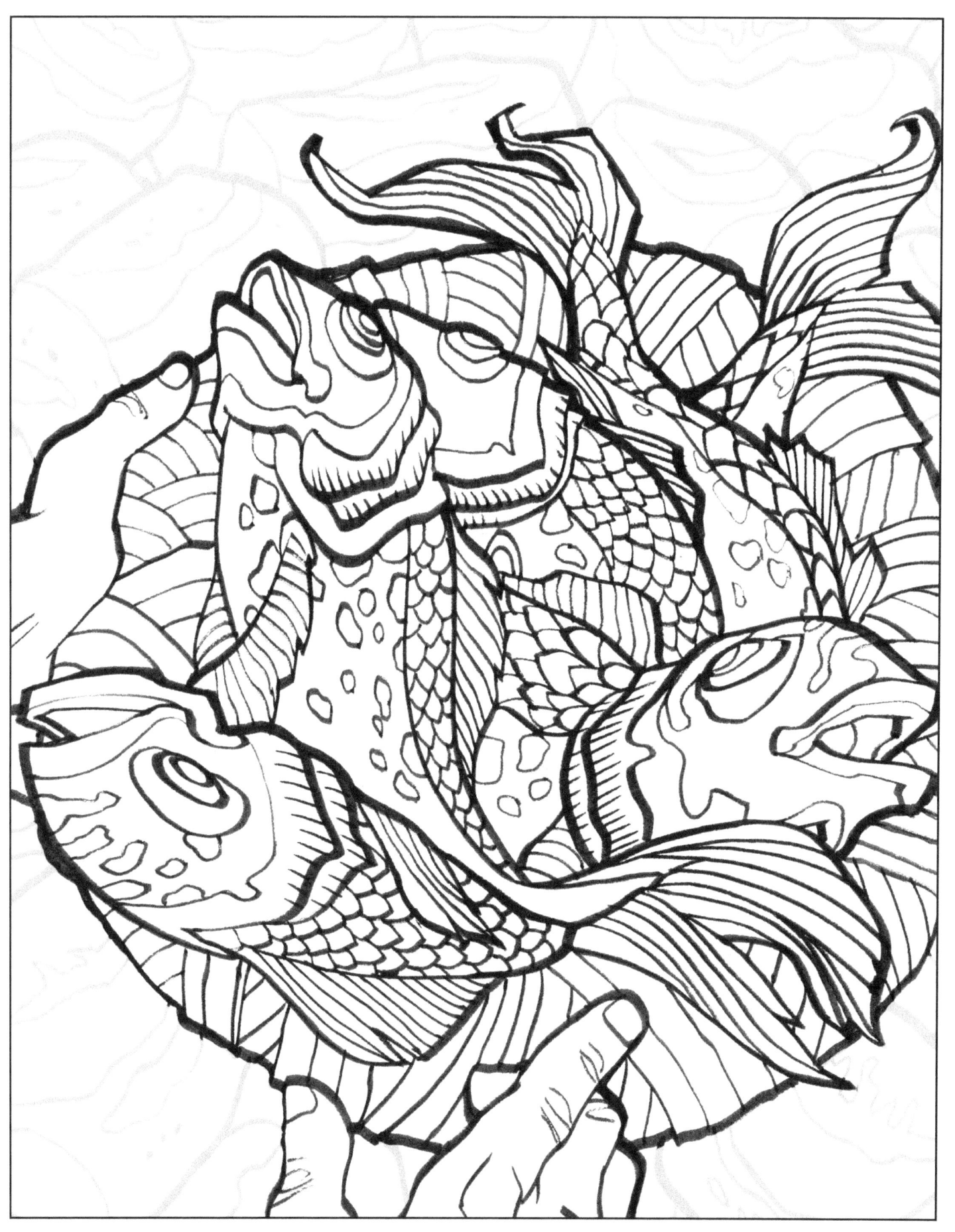

THE LOAVES AND FISHES

Matthew 14:16
King James Bible

But Jesus said unto them, They need not depart; give ye them to eat.

And they say unto him, We have here but five loaves, and two fishes.

He said, Bring them hither to me.

And he commanded the multitude to sit down on the grass, and took the five loaves, and the two fishes, and looking up to heaven, he blessed, and brake, and gave the loaves to his disciples, and the disciples to the multitude.

And they did all eat, and were filled: and they took up of the fragments that remained twelve baskets full.

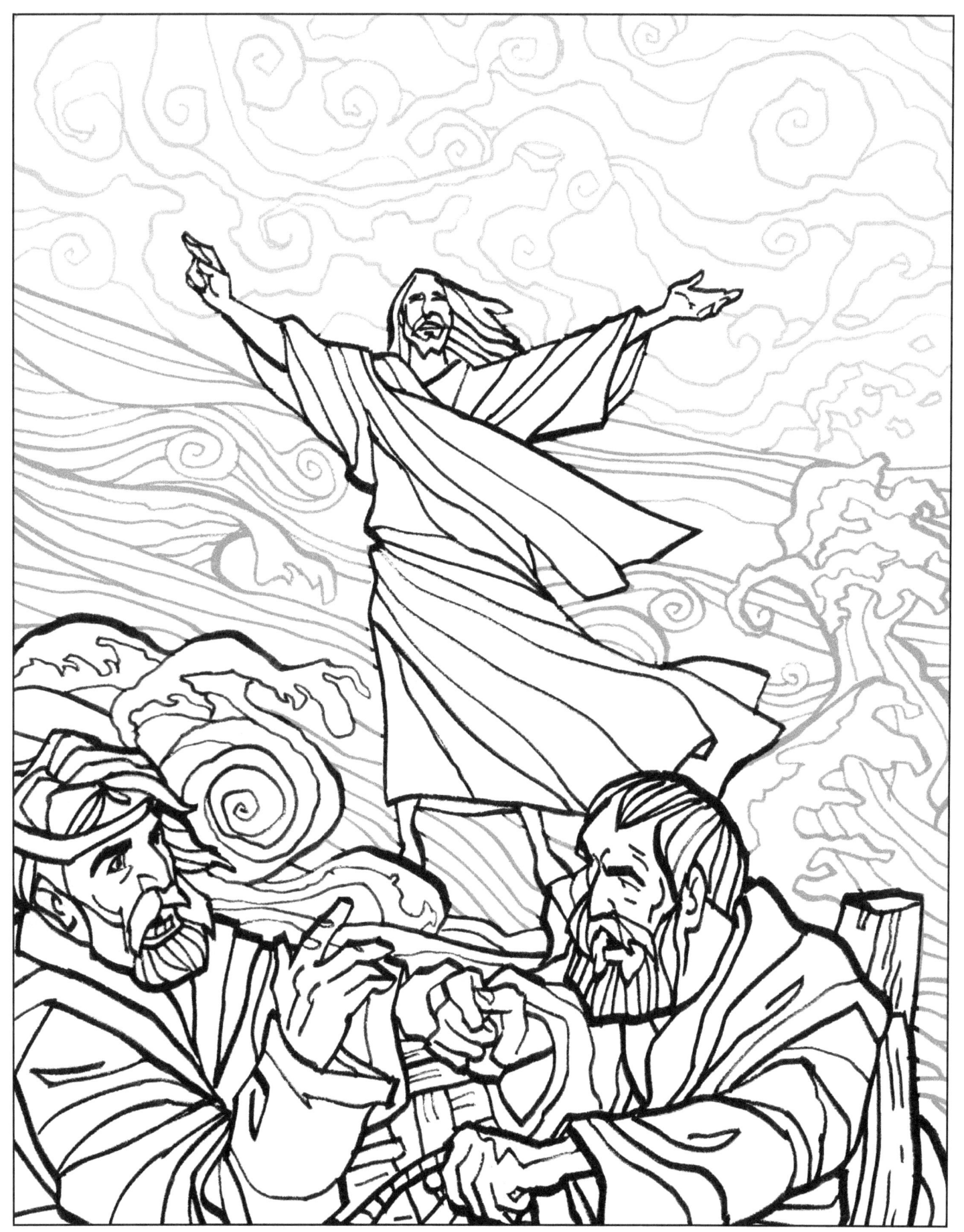

JESUS WALKS ON WATER

Matthew 14:24
King James Bible

But the ship was now in the midst of the sea, tossed with waves: for the wind was contrary. And in the fourth watch of the night Jesus went unto them, walking on the sea.

And when the disciples saw him walking on the sea, they were troubled, saying, It is a spirit; and they cried out for fear.

But straightway Jesus spake unto them, saying, Be of good cheer; it is I; be not afraid.

And Peter answered him and said, Lord, if it be thou, bid me come unto thee on the water.

And he said, Come. And when Peter was come down out of the ship, he walked on the water, to go to Jesus.

But when he saw the wind boisterous, he was afraid; and beginning to sink, he cried, saying, Lord, save me.

And immediately Jesus stretched forth his hand, and caught him, and said unto him, O thou of little faith, wherefore didst thou doubt?

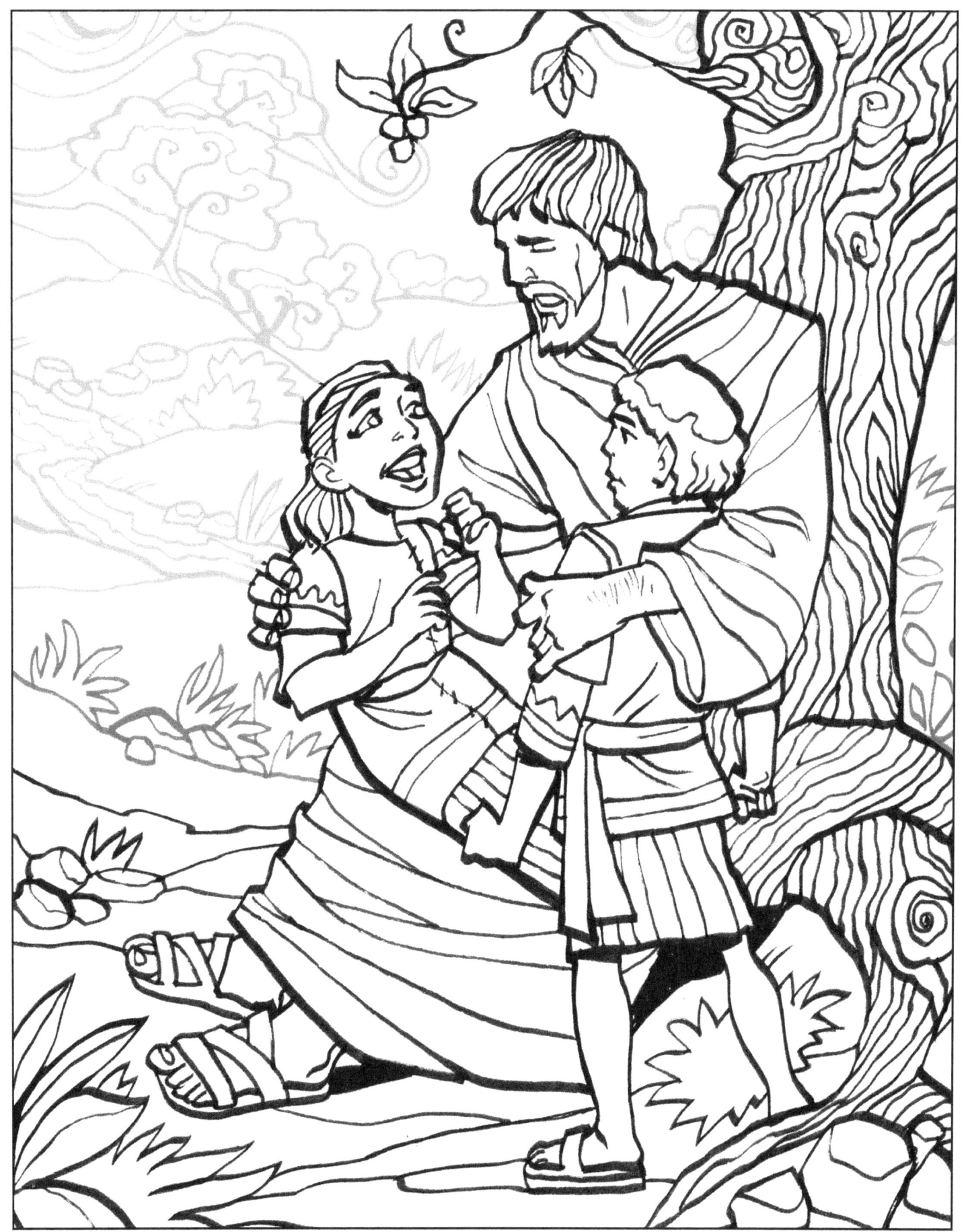

COME UNTO ME

Matthew 19:14

King James Bible

But Jesus said, Suffer little children, and forbid them not, to come unto me: for of such is the kingdom of heaven.

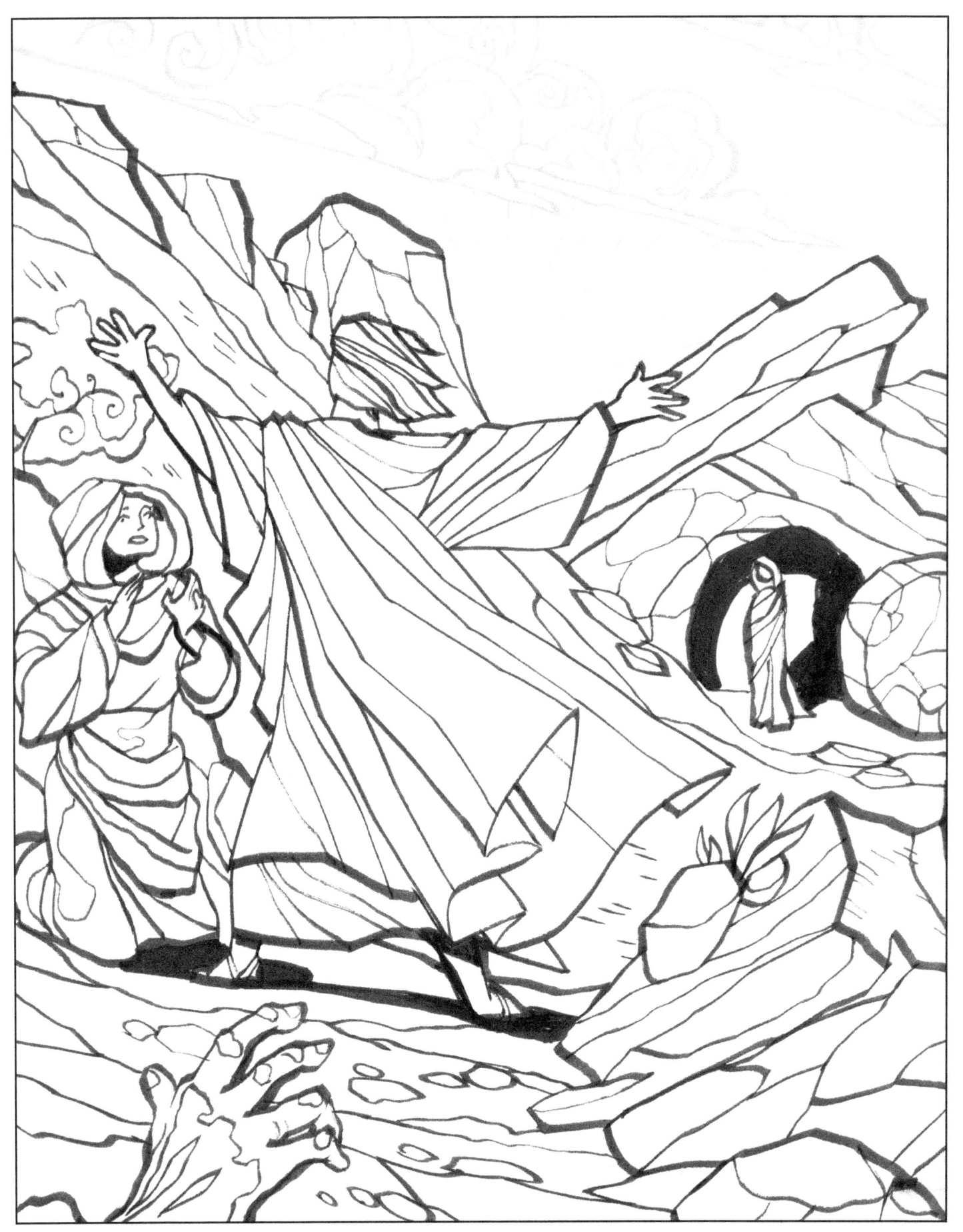

JESUS CALLS LAZURUS FROM THE GRAVE

John 11:23-27

King James Bible

Jesus saith unto her, Thy brother shall rise again.

Martha saith unto him, I know that he shall rise again in the resurrection at the last day.

Jesus said unto her, I am the resurrection, and the life: he that believeth in me, though he were dead, yet shall he live:

And whosoever liveth and believeth in me shall never die. Believest thou this?

She saith unto him, Yea, Lord: I believe that thou art the Christ, the Son of God, which should come into the world.

John 11:40-44

Jesus saith unto her, Said I not unto thee, that, if thou wouldest believe, thou shouldest see the glory of God?

Then they took away the stone from the place where the dead was laid. And Jesus lifted up his eyes, and said, Father, I thank thee that thou hast heard me.

And I knew that thou hearest me always: but because of the people which stand by I said it, that they may believe that thou hast sent me.

And when he thus had spoken, he cried with a loud voice, Lazarus, come forth.

And he that was dead came forth, bound hand and foot with graveclothes: and his face was bound about with a napkin. Jesus saith unto them, Loose him, and let him go.

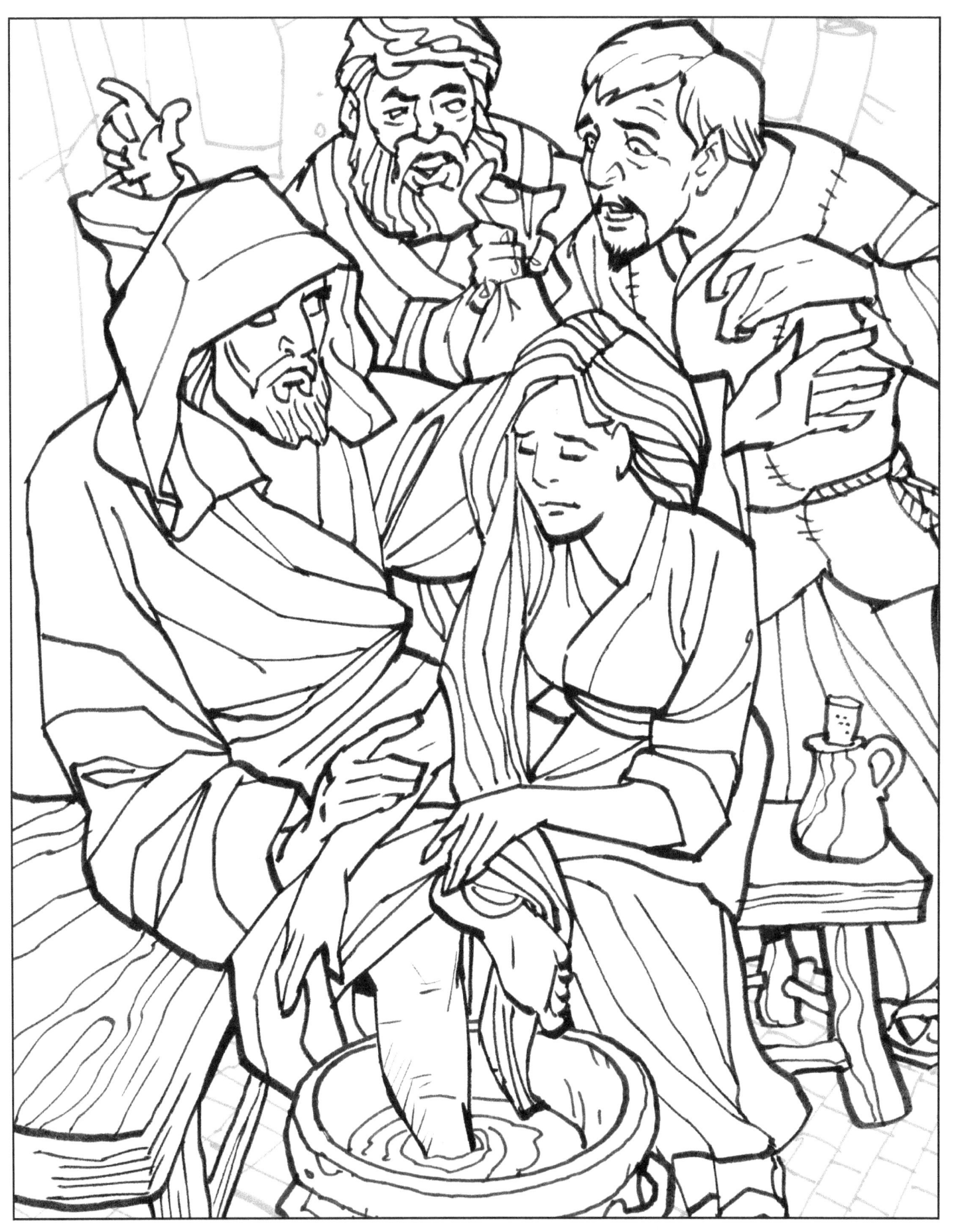

MARY ANOINTS THE FEET OF JESUS

John 12:1
King James Bible

Then Jesus six days before the passover came to Bethany, where Lazarus was, which had been dead, whom he raised from the dead.

There they made him a supper; and Martha served: but Lazarus was one of them that sat at the table with him.

Then took Mary a pound of ointment of spikenard, very costly, and anointed the feet of Jesus, and wiped his feet with her hair: and the house was filled with the odour of the ointment.

Then saith one of his disciples, Judas Iscariot, Simon's son, which should betray him,

Why was not this ointment sold for three hundred pence, and given to the poor?

This he said, not that he cared for the poor; but because he was a thief, and had the bag, and bare what was put therein.

Then said Jesus, Let her alone: against the day of my burying hath she kept this.

For the poor always ye have with you; but me ye have not always.

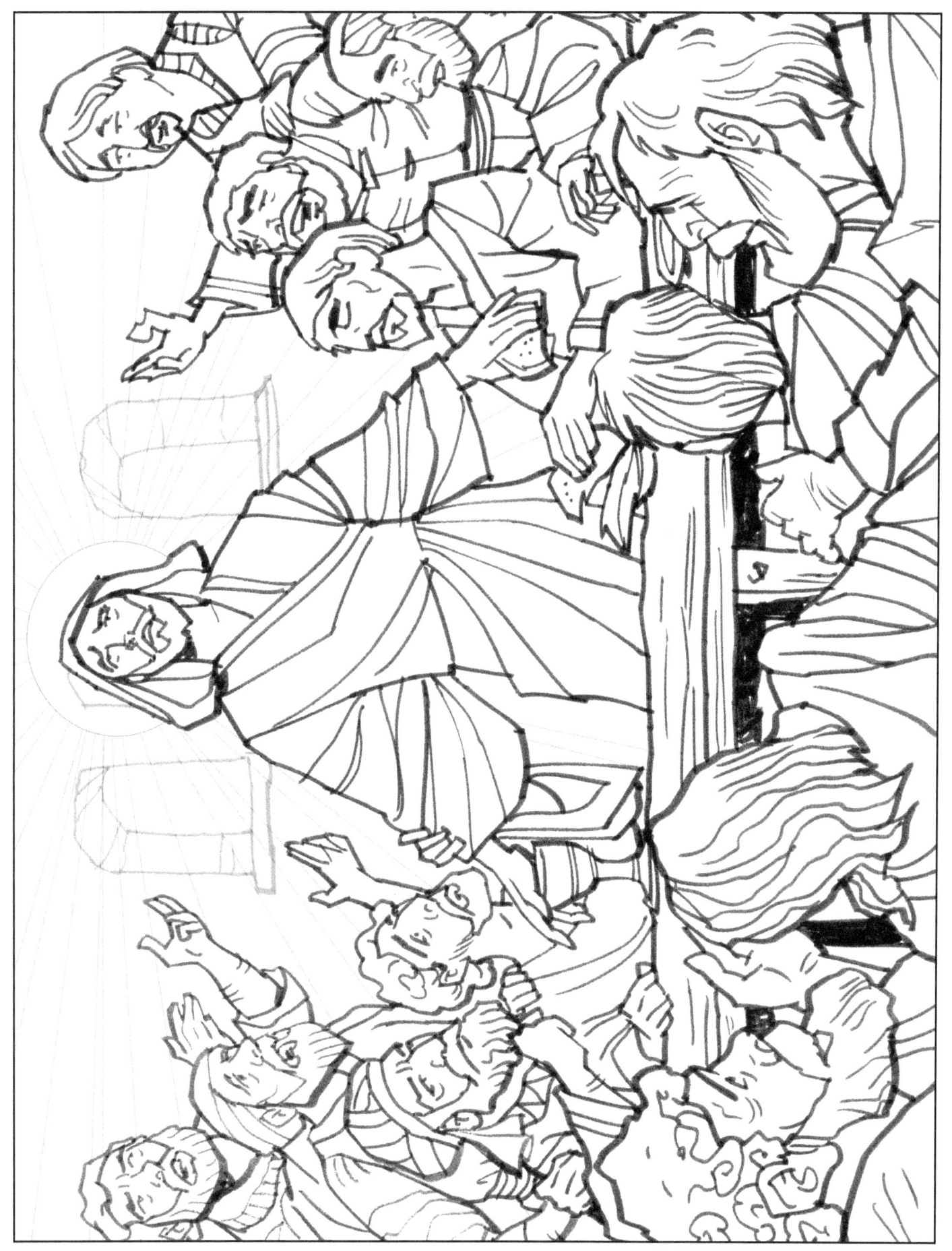

A New Covenant is Made

Matthew 26:26
King James Bible

And as they were eating, Jesus took bread, and blessed it, and brake it, and gave it to the disciples, and said, Take, eat; this is my body.

And he took the cup, and gave thanks, and gave it to them, saying, Drink ye all of it;

For this is my blood of the new testament, which is shed for many for the remission of sins.

But I say unto you, I will not drink henceforth of this fruit of the vine, until that day when I drink it new with you in my Father's kingdom.

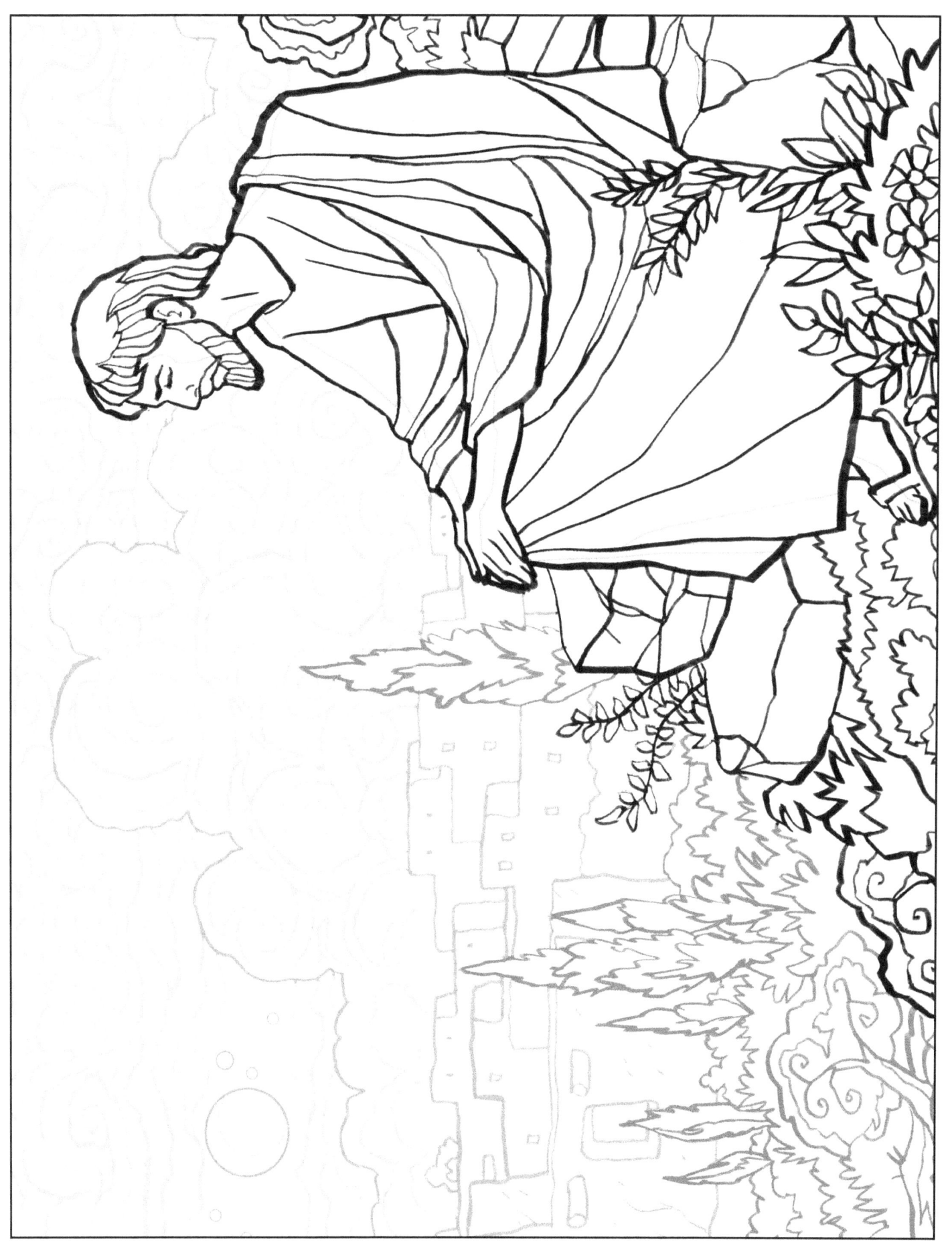

JESUS PRAYS IN THE GARDEN

Matthew 26:36
King James Bible

Then cometh Jesus with them unto a place called Gethsemane, and saith unto the disciples, Sit ye here, while I go and pray yonder.

And he took with him Peter and the two sons of Zebedee, and began to be sorrowful and very heavy.

Then saith he unto them, My soul is exceeding sorrowful, even unto death: tarry ye here, and watch with me.

And he went a little farther, and fell on his face, and prayed, saying, O my Father, if it be possible, let this cup pass from me: nevertheless not as I will, but as thou wilt.

And he cometh unto the disciples, and findeth them asleep, and saith unto Peter, What, could ye not watch with me one hour?

Watch and pray, that ye enter not into temptation: the spirit indeed is willing, but the flesh is weak.

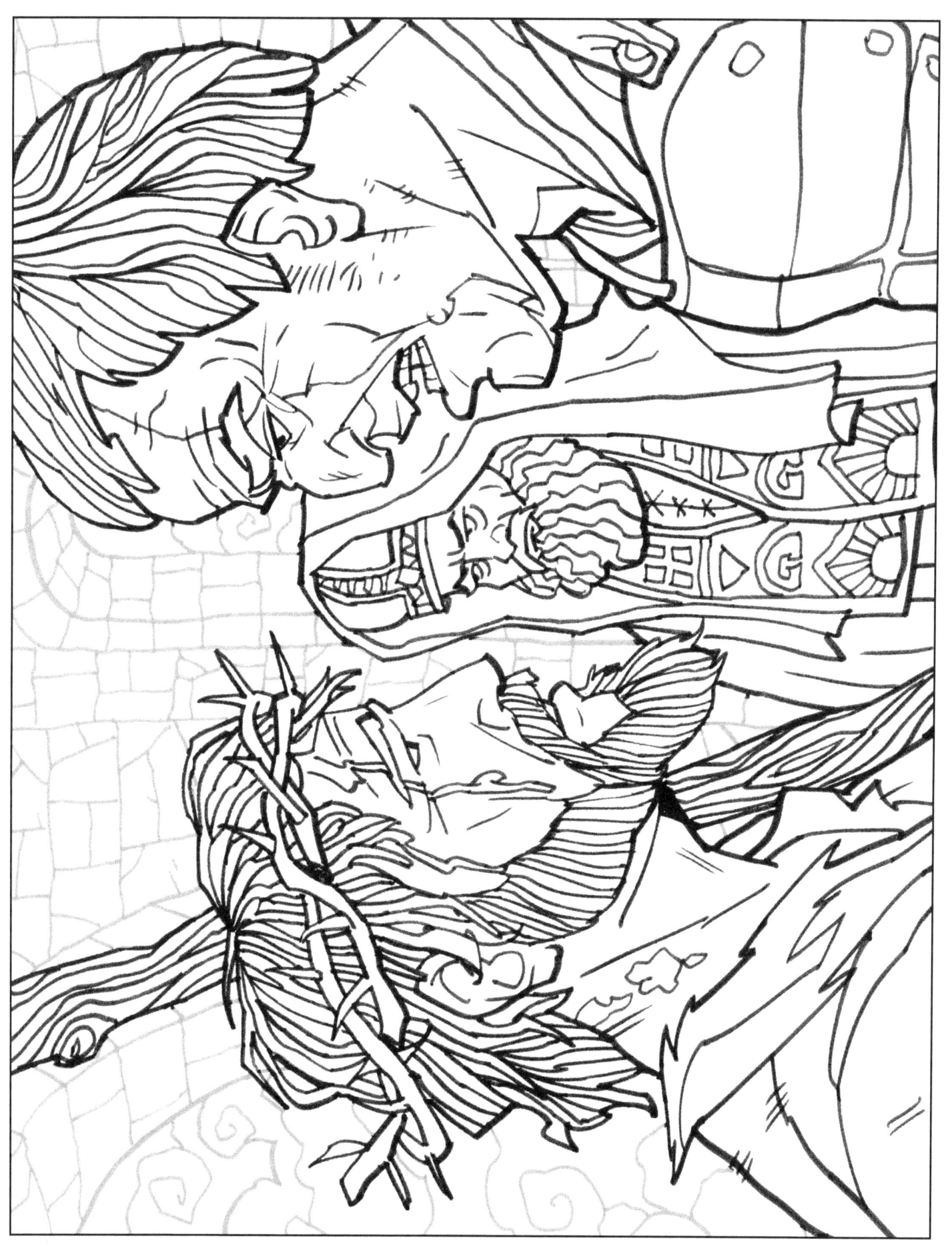

They Delivered Jesus Unto Pontius Pilate

Luke 22:66
King James Bible

And as soon as it was day, the elders of the people and the chief priests and the scribes came together, and led him into their council, saying,

Art thou the Christ? tell us. And he said unto them, If I tell you, ye will not believe:

And if I also ask you, ye will not answer me, nor let me go.

Hereafter shall the Son of man sit on the right hand of the power of God.

Then said they all, Art thou then the Son of God? And he said unto them, Ye say that I am.

Matthew 27:1

When the morning was come, all the chief priests and elders of the people took counsel against Jesus to put him to death:

And when they had bound him, they led him away, and delivered him to Pontius Pilate the governor.

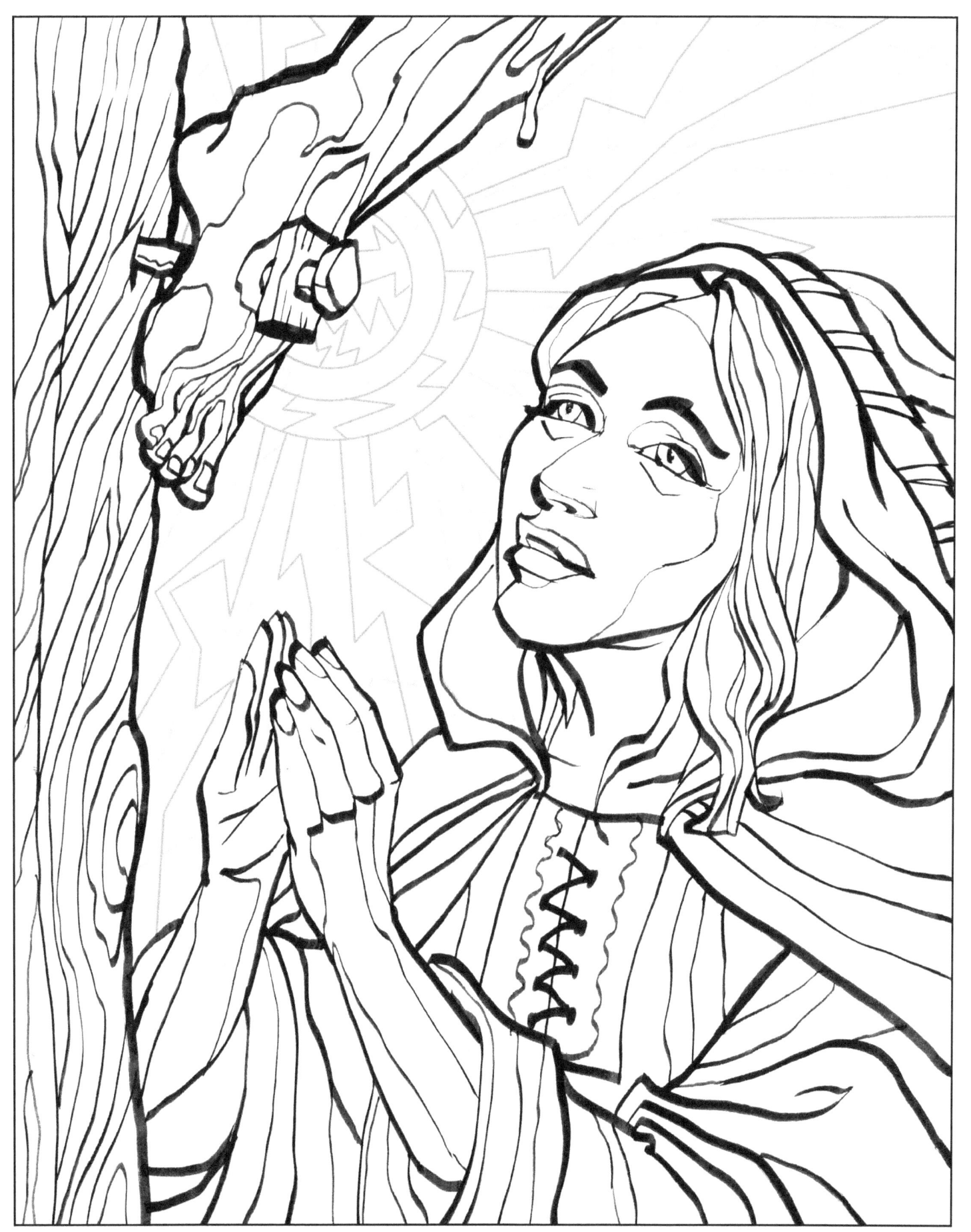

JESUS IS CRUCIFIED FOR THE SINS OF THE WORLD

LUKE 23:39

King James Bible

And one of the malefactors which were hanged railed on him, saying, If thou be Christ, save thyself and us.

But the other answering rebuked him, saying, Dost not thou fear God, seeing thou art in the same condemnation?

And we indeed justly; for we receive the due reward of our deeds: but this man hath done nothing amiss.

And he said unto Jesus, Lord, remember me when thou comest into thy kingdom.

And Jesus said unto him, Verily I say unto thee, Today shalt thou be with me in paradise.

And it was about the sixth hour, and there was a darkness over all the earth until the ninth hour.

And the sun was darkened, and the veil of the temple was rent in the midst.

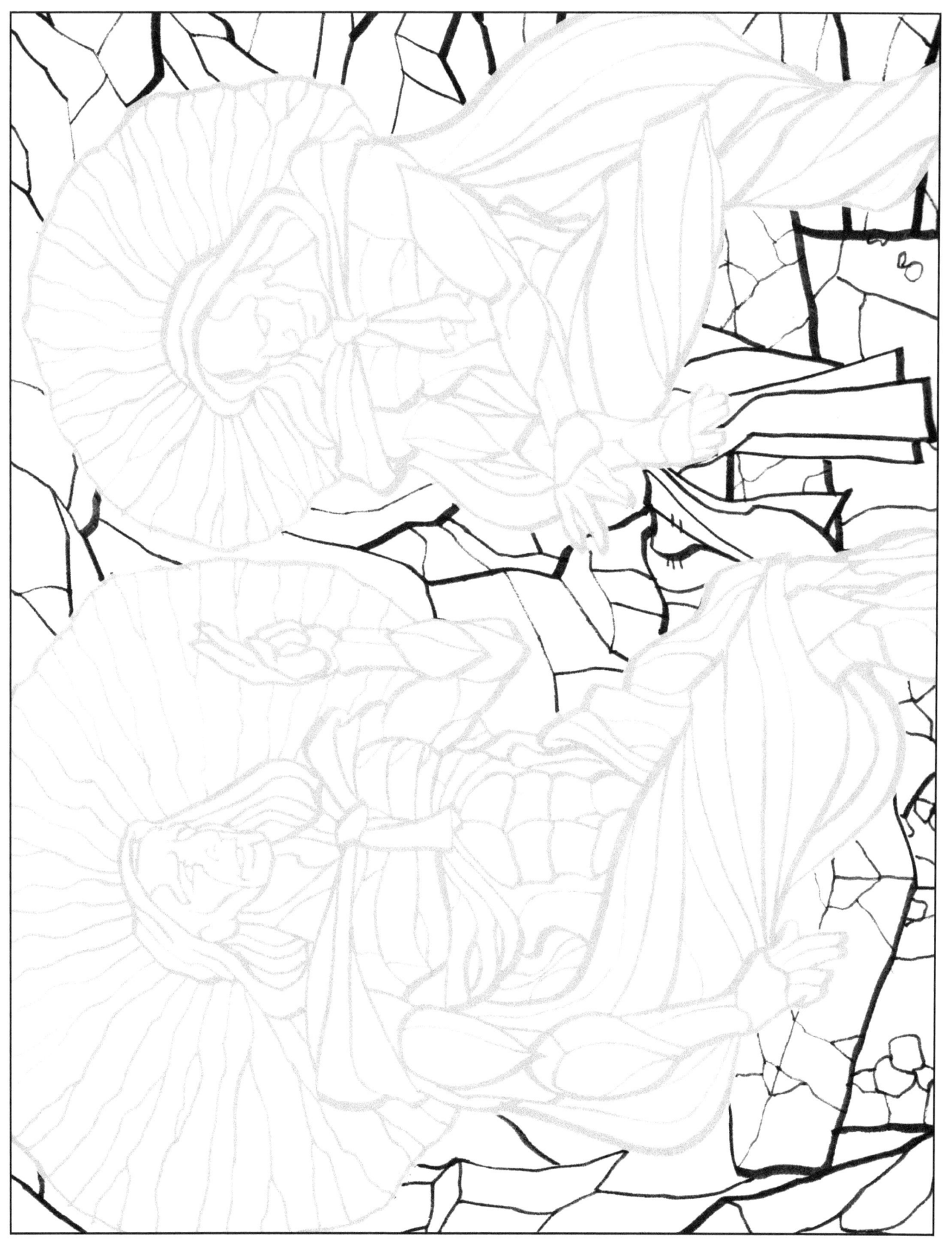

ANGELS IN THE EMPTY TOMB

John 20:9

King James Bible

For as yet they knew not the scripture, that he must rise again from the dead.

Then the disciples went away again unto their own home.

But Mary stood without at the sepulchre weeping: and as she wept, she stooped down, and looked into the sepulchre,

And seeth two angels in white sitting, the one at the head, and the other at the feet, where the body of Jesus had lain.

And they say unto her, Woman, why weepest thou? She saith unto them, Because they have taken away my Lord, and I know not where they have laid him.

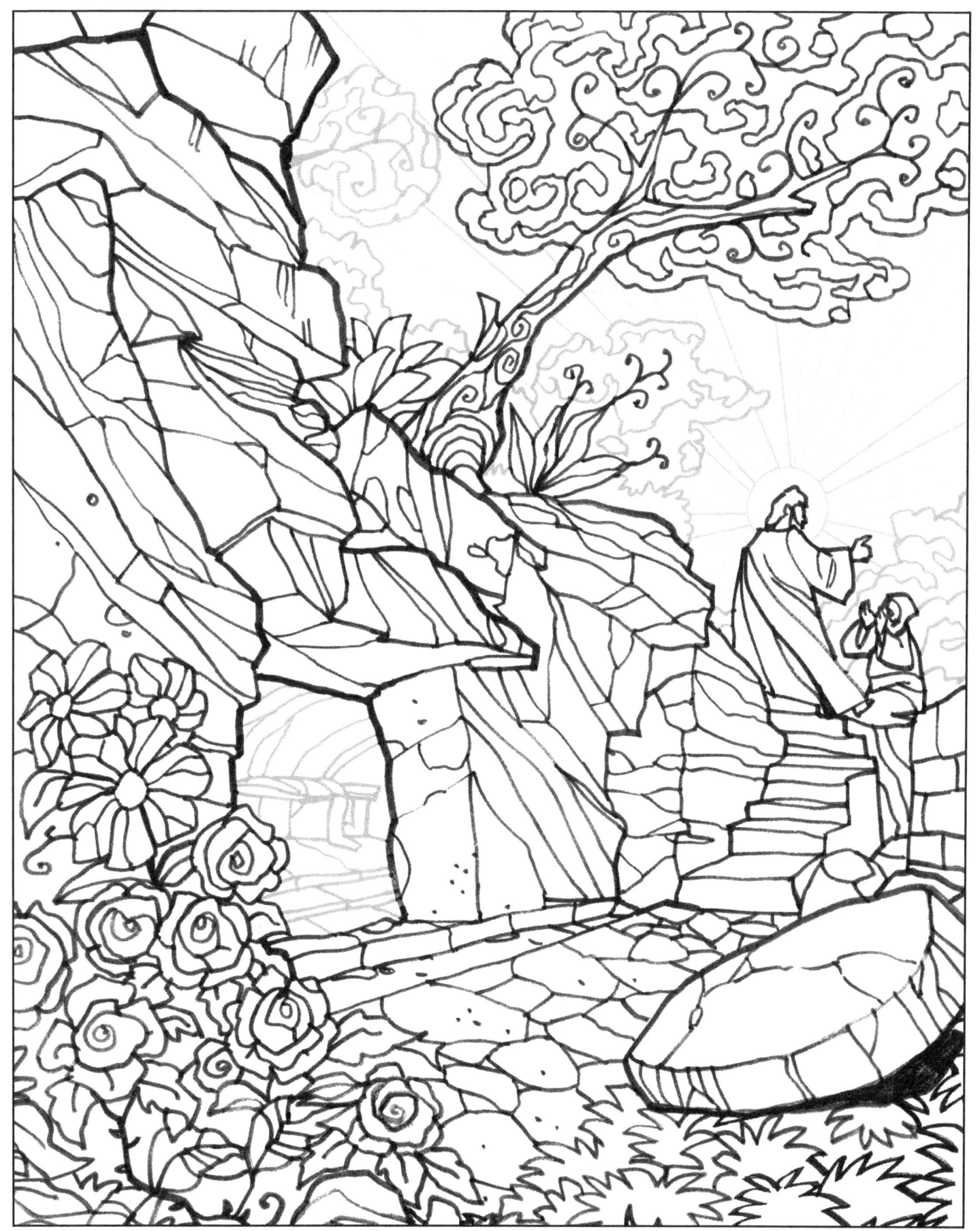

Jesus is Risen!

John 20:14
King James Bible

And when she had thus said, she turned herself back, and saw Jesus standing, and knew not that it was Jesus.

Jesus saith unto her, Woman, why weepest thou? whom seekest thou? She, supposing him to be the gardener, saith unto him, Sir, if thou have borne him hence, tell me where thou hast laid him, and I will take him away.

Jesus saith unto her, Mary. She turned herself, and saith unto him, Rabboni; which is to say, Master.

Jesus saith unto her, Touch me not; for I am not yet ascended to my Father: but go to my brethren, and say unto them, I ascend unto my Father, and your Father; and to my God, and your God.

Mary Magdalene came and told the disciples that she had seen the Lord, and that he had spoken these things unto her.

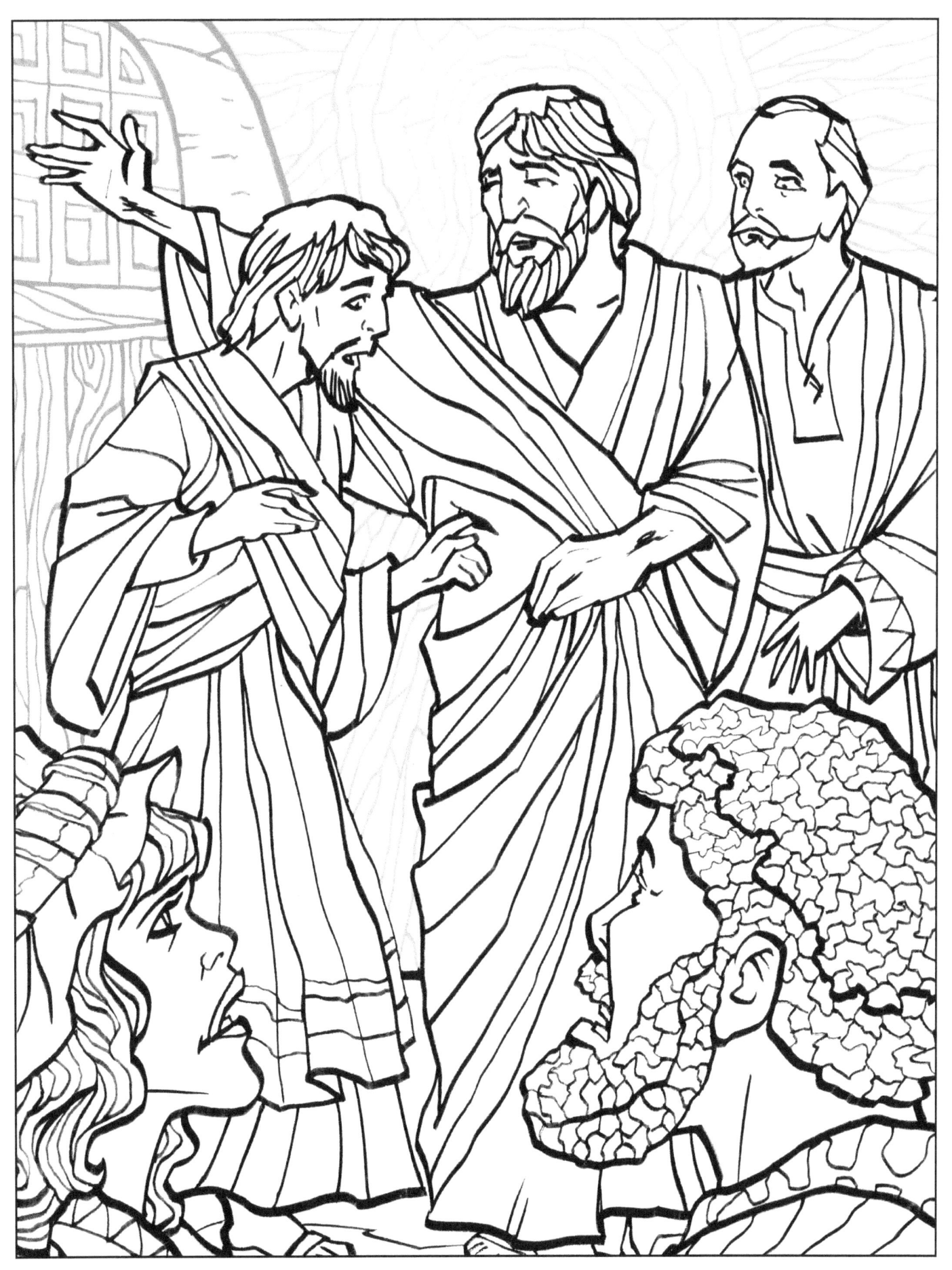

Thomas Must See Christ's Wounds To Believe

John 20:26
King James Bible

And after eight days again his disciples were within, and Thomas with them: then came Jesus, the doors being shut, and stood in the midst, and said, Peace be unto you.

Then saith he to Thomas, Reach hither thy finger, and behold my hands; and reach hither thy hand, and thrust it into my side: and be not faithless, but believing.

And Thomas answered and said unto him, My Lord and my God.

Jesus saith unto him, Thomas, because thou hast seen me, thou hast believed: blessed are they that have not seen, and yet have believed.

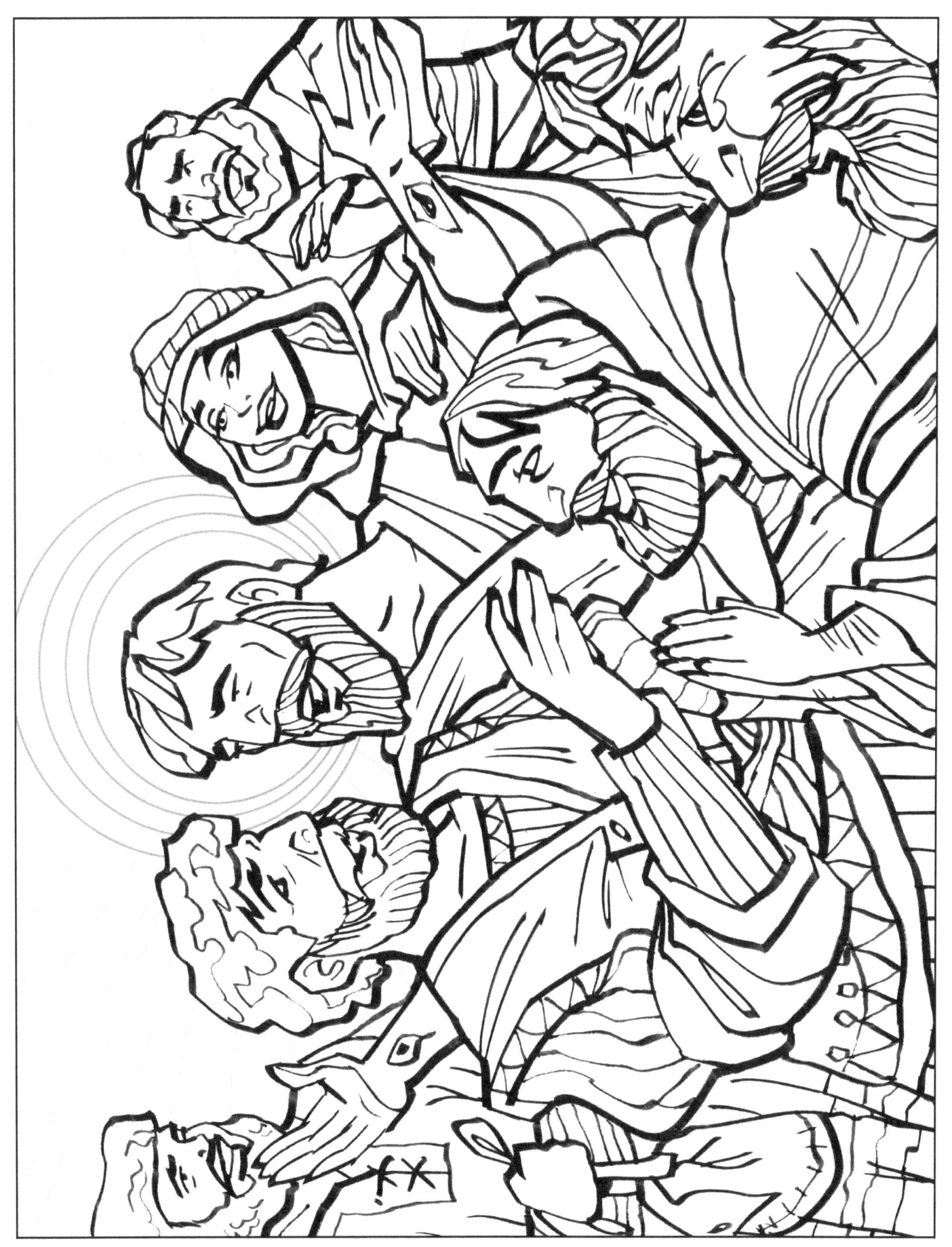

I Am With You Always

Matthew 28:18
King James Bible

And Jesus came and spake unto them, saying, All power is given unto me in heaven and in earth.

Go ye therefore, and teach all nations, baptizing them in the name of the Father, and of the Son, and of the Holy Ghost:

Teaching them to observe all things whatsoever I have commanded you: and, lo, I am with you always, even unto the end of the world. Amen.

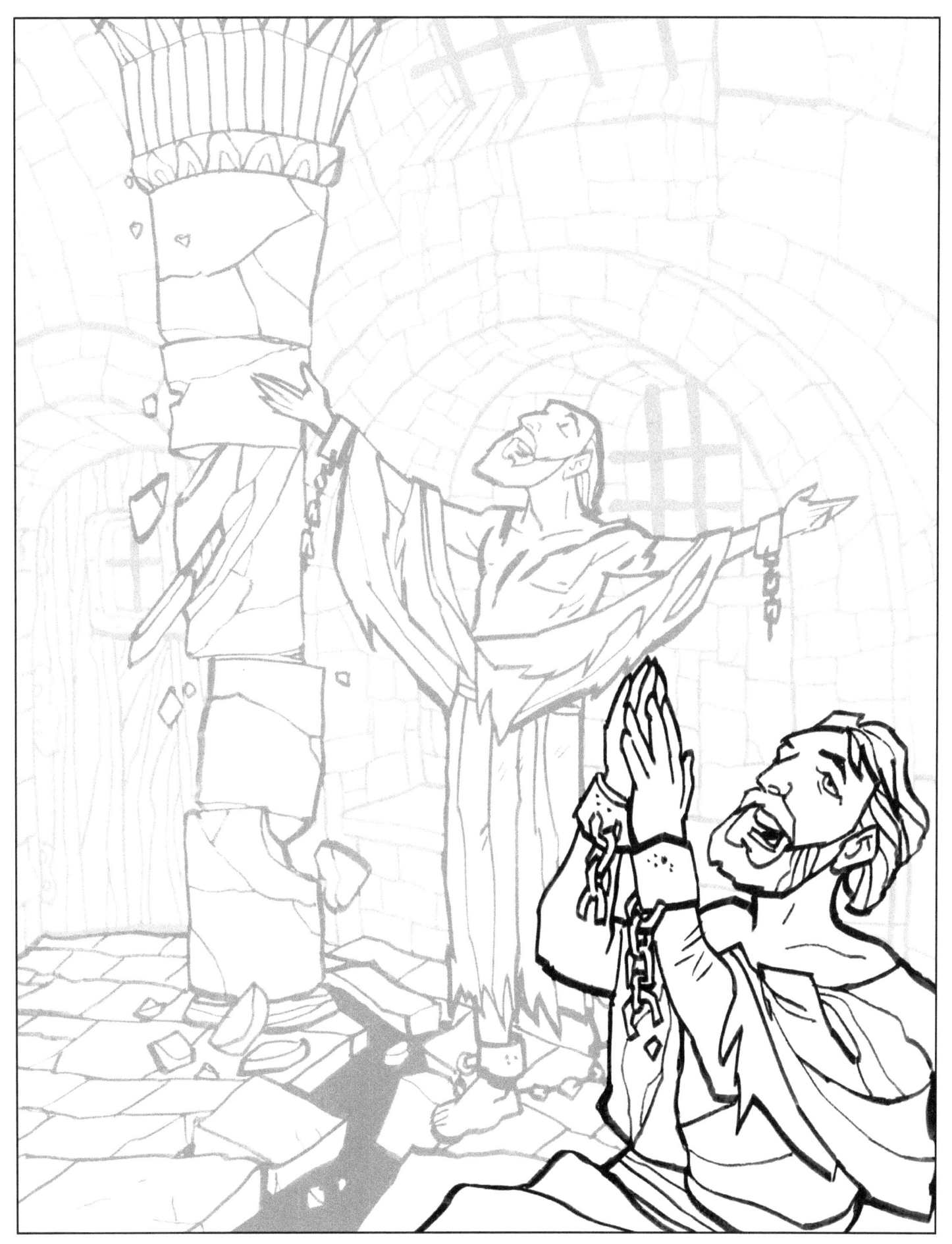

PAUL PRAISES THE LORD WHILE IN BONDAGE

Acts 16:23
King James Bible

And when they had laid many stripes upon them, they cast them into prison, charging the jailor to keep them safely:

Who, having received such a charge, thrust them into the inner prison, and made their feet fast in the stocks.

And at midnight Paul and Silas prayed, and sang praises unto God: and the prisoners heard them.

And suddenly there was a great earthquake, so that the foundations of the prison were shaken: and immediately all the doors were opened, and every one's bands were loosed.

And the keeper of the prison awaking out of his sleep, and seeing the prison doors open, he drew out his sword, and would have killed himself, supposing that the prisoners had been fled.

But Paul cried with a loud voice, saying, Do thyself no harm: for we are all here.

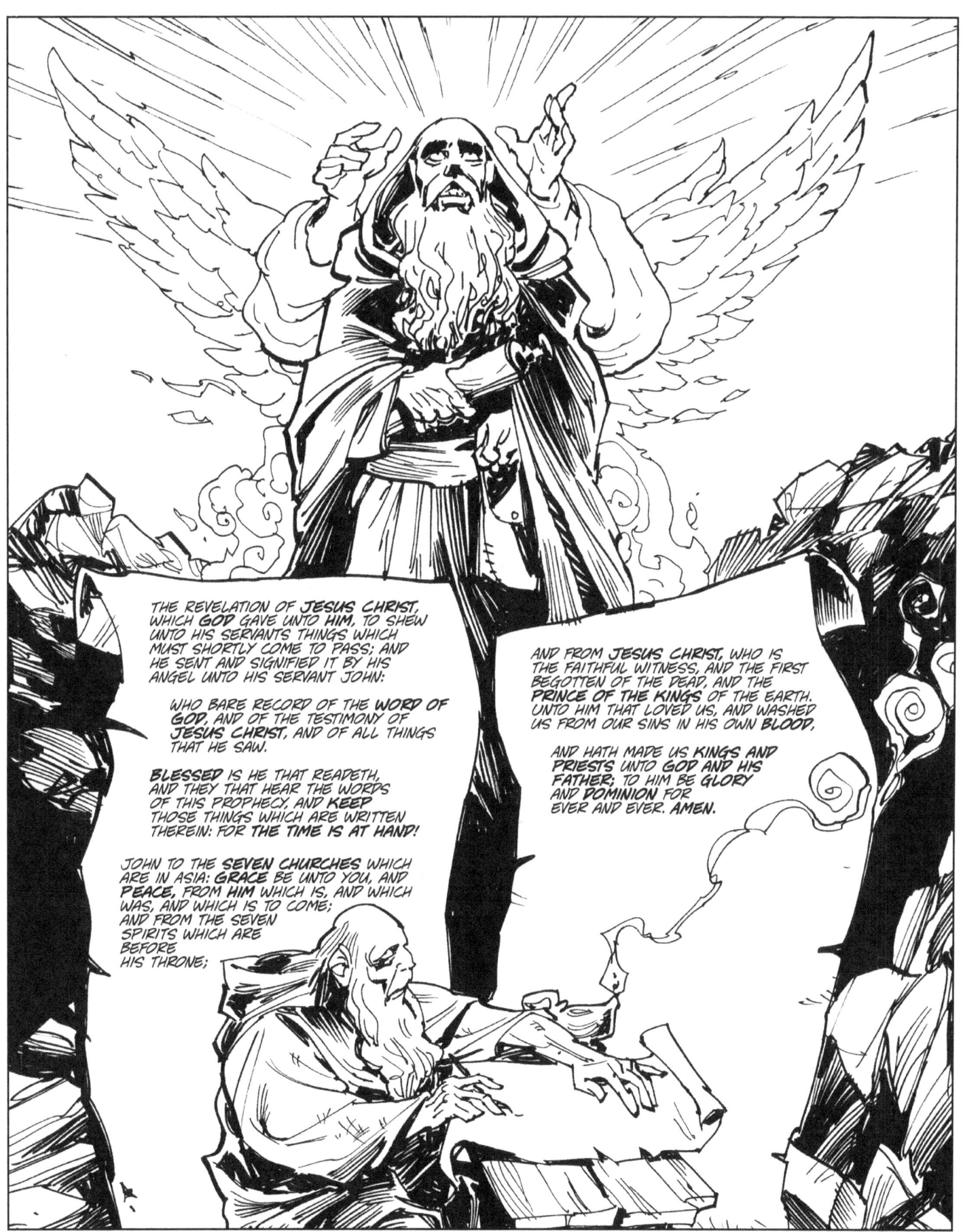

THE REVELATION OF JESUS CHRIST TO JOHN
(Art from the new Revelation Graphic Novel)

Revelation 1:1
King James Bible

The Revelation of Jesus Christ, which God gave unto him, to shew unto his servants things which must shortly come to pass; and he sent and signified it by his angel unto his servant John:

Who bare record of the word of God, and of the testimony of Jesus Christ, and of all things that he saw.

Blessed is he that readeth, and they that hear the words of this prophecy, and keep those things which are written therein: for the time is at hand.

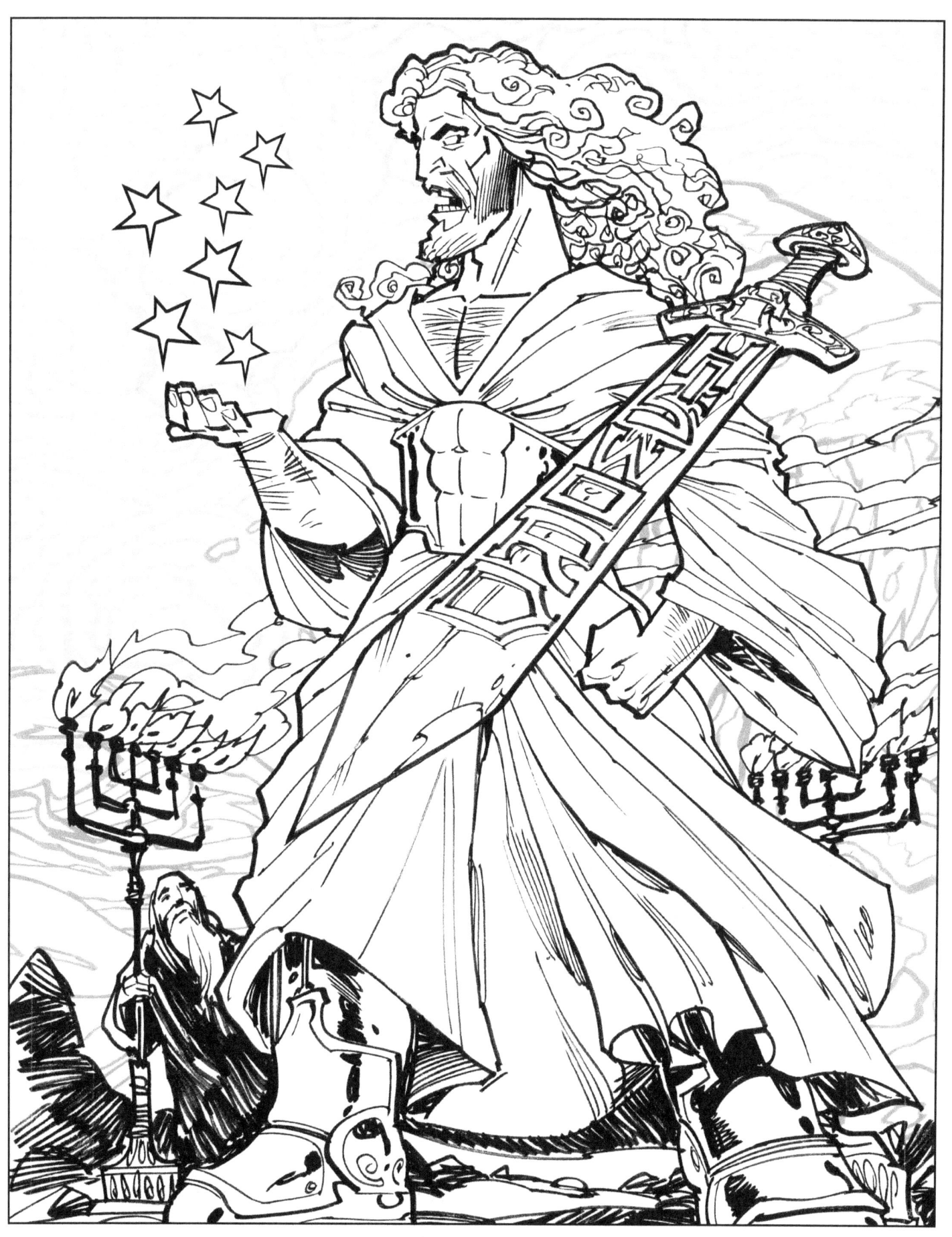

I Am Alive For Evermore
(Art from the new Revelation Graphic Novel)

REVELATION 1:12
King James Bible

And I turned to see the voice that spake with me. And being turned, I saw seven golden candlesticks;

And in the midst of the seven candlesticks one like unto the Son of man, clothed with a garment down to the foot, and girt about the paps with a golden girdle.

His head and his hairs were white like wool, as white as snow; and his eyes were as a flame of fire;

And his feet like unto fine brass, as if they burned in a furnace; and his voice as the sound of many waters.

And he had in his right hand seven stars: and out of his mouth went a sharp twoedged sword: and his countenance was as the sun shineth in his strength.

And when I saw him, I fell at his feet as dead. And he laid his right hand upon me, saying unto me, Fear not; I am the first and the last:

I am he that liveth, and was dead; and, behold, I am alive for evermore, Amen; and have the keys of hell and of death.

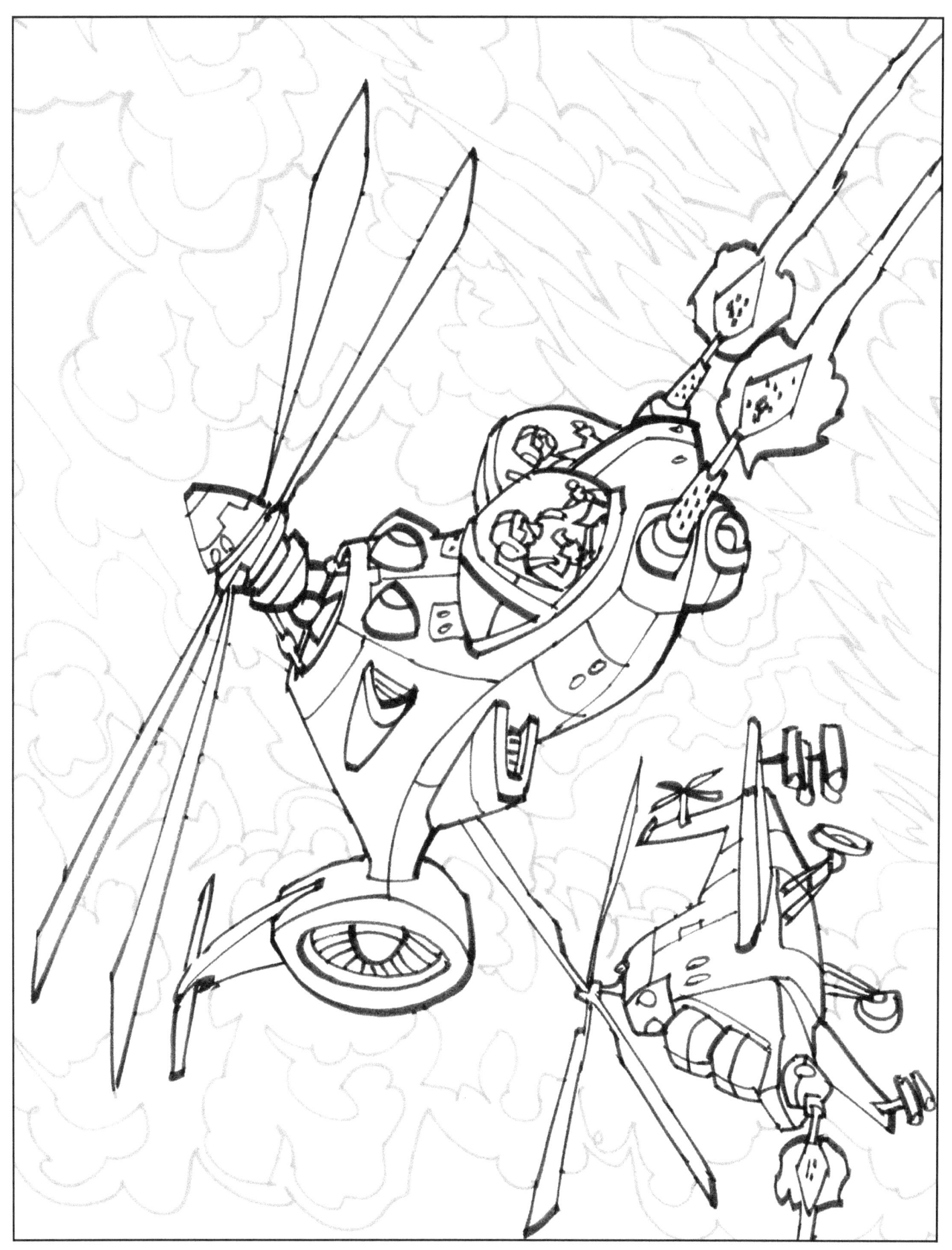

THE FACES OF THE LOCUSTS WERE LIKE FACES OF MEN

Revelation 9:7
King James Bible

The shape of the locusts was like horses prepared for battle. On their heads were crowns of something like gold, and their faces were like the faces of men.

They had hair like women's hair, and their teeth were like lions' teeth.

And they had breastplates like breastplates of iron, and the sound of their wings was like the sound of chariots with many horses running into battle.

They had tails like scorpions, and there were stings in their tails.

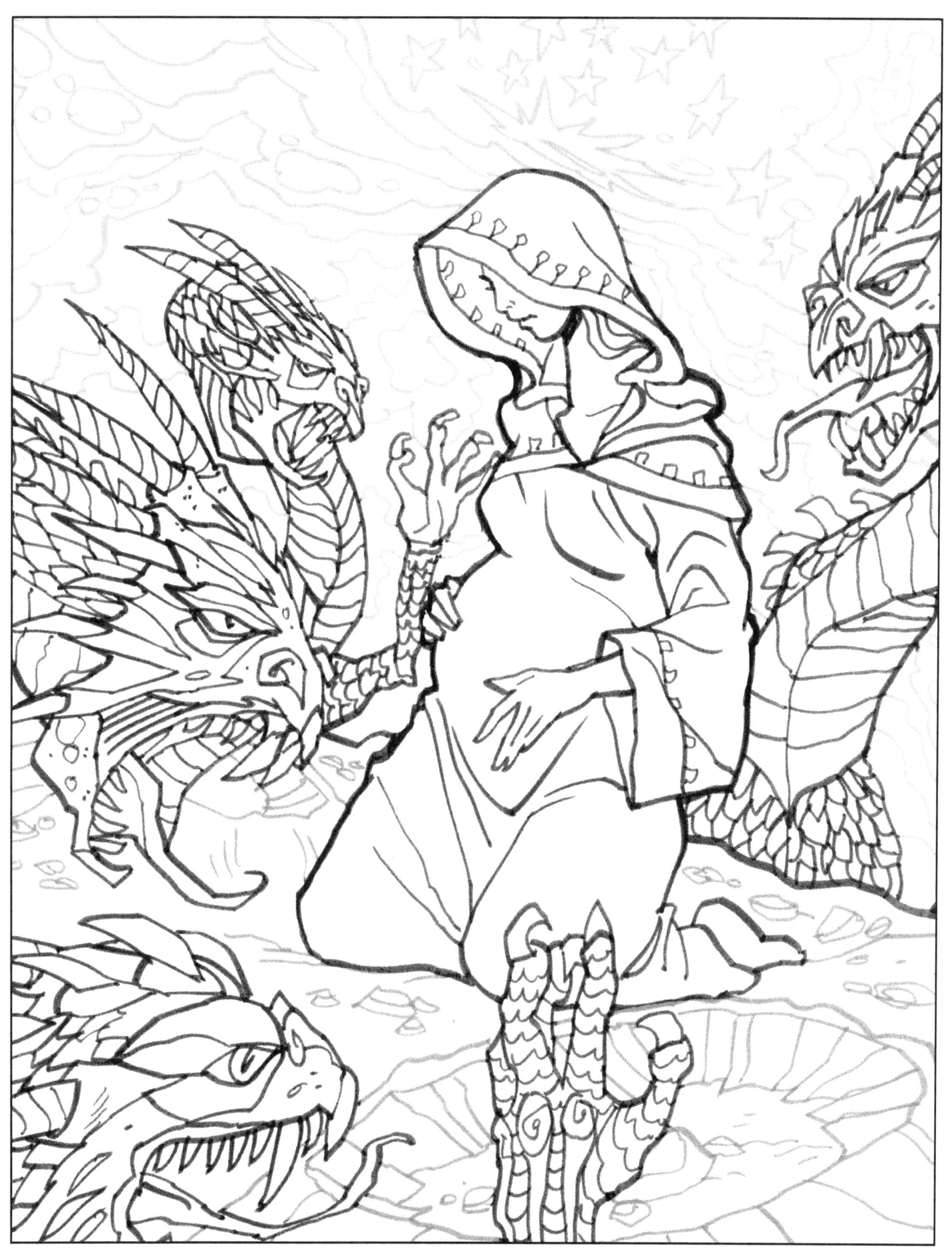

A Great Wonder in Heaven

Revelation 12:1
King James Bible

And there appeared a great wonder in heaven; a woman clothed with the sun, and the moon under her feet, and upon her head a crown of twelve stars:

And she being with child cried, travailing in birth, and pained to be delivered.

And there appeared another wonder in heaven; and behold a great red dragon, having seven heads and ten horns, and seven crowns upon his heads.

And his tail drew the third part of the stars of heaven, and did cast them to the earth: and the dragon stood before the woman which was ready to be delivered, for to devour her child as soon as it was born.

And she brought forth a man child, who was to rule all nations with a rod of iron: and her child was caught up unto God, and to his throne.

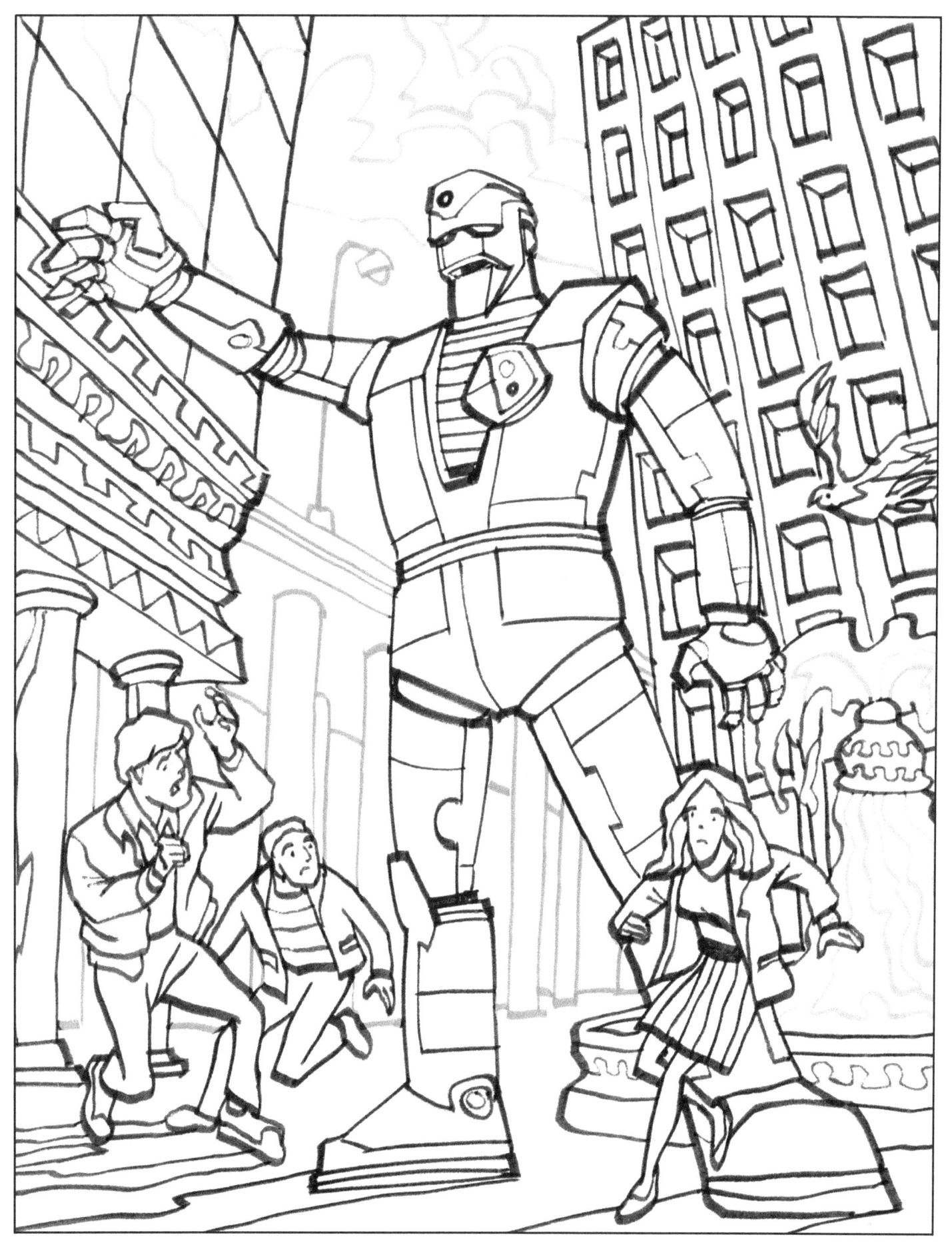

He Had Power To Give Life To The Image Of The Beast

Revelation 13:11

King James Bible

And I beheld another beast coming up out of the earth; and he had two horns like a lamb, and he spake as a dragon.

And he exerciseth all the power of the first beast before him, and causeth the earth and them which dwell therein to worship the first beast, whose deadly wound was healed.

And he doeth great wonders, so that he maketh fire come down from heaven on the earth in the sight of men,

And deceiveth them that dwell on the earth by the means of those miracles which he had power to do in the sight of the beast; saying to them that dwell on the earth, that they should make an image to the beast, which had the wound by a sword, and did live.

And he had power to give life unto the image of the beast, that the image of the beast should both speak, and cause that as many as would not worship the image of the beast should be killed.

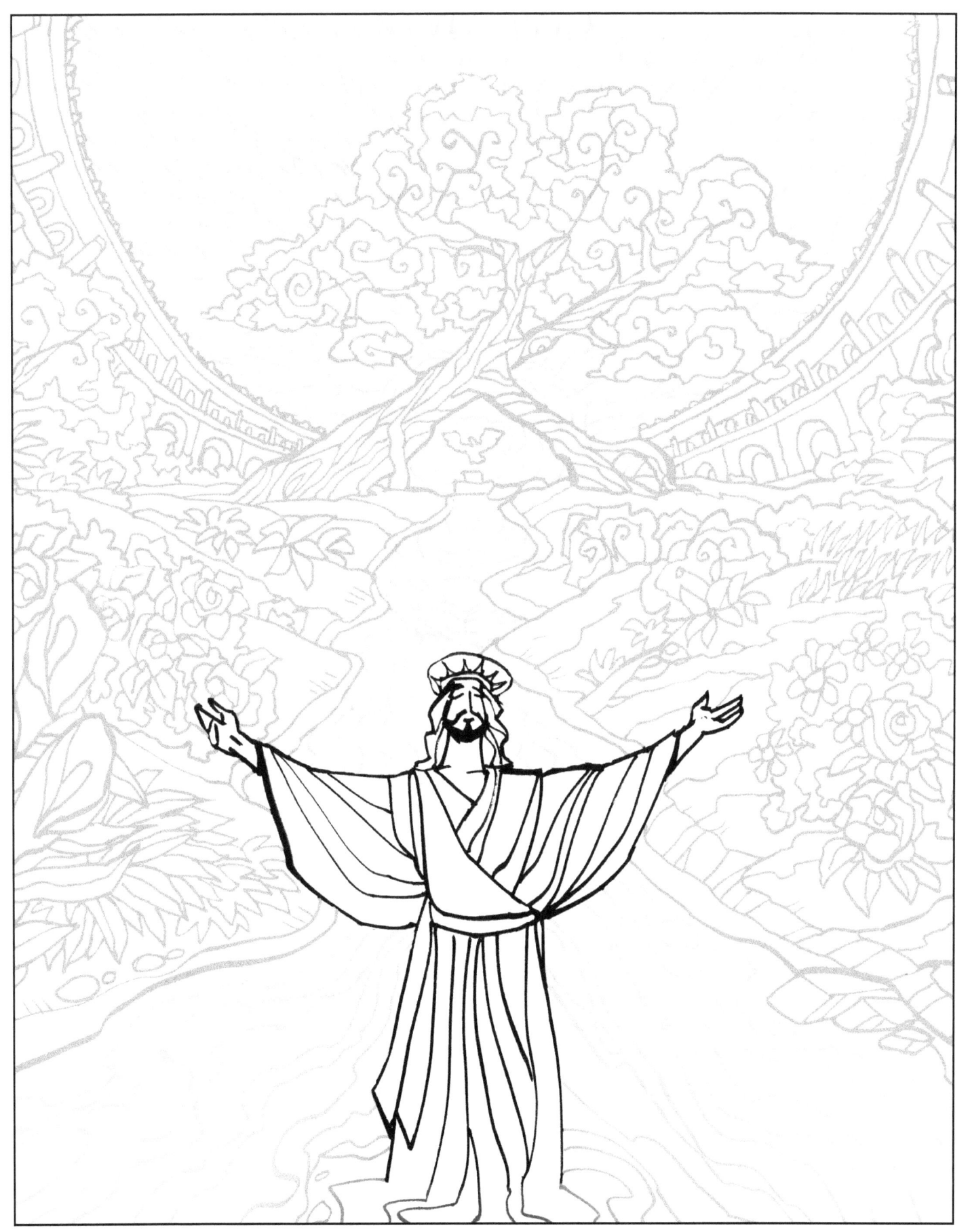

I AM ALPHA AND OMEGA

REVELATION 22:1
KING JAMES BIBLE

AND HE SHEWED ME A PURE RIVER OF WATER OF LIFE, CLEAR AS CRYSTAL, PROCEEDING OUT OF THE THRONE OF GOD AND OF THE LAMB.

IN THE MIDST OF THE STREET OF IT, AND ON EITHER SIDE OF THE RIVER, WAS THERE THE TREE OF LIFE, WHICH BARE TWELVE MANNER OF FRUITS, AND YIELDED HER FRUIT EVERY MONTH: AND THE LEAVES OF THE TREE WERE FOR THE HEALING OF THE NATIONS.

AND THERE SHALL BE NO MORE CURSE: BUT THE THRONE OF GOD AND OF THE LAMB SHALL BE IN IT; AND HIS SERVANTS SHALL SERVE HIM:

AND THEY SHALL SEE HIS FACE; AND HIS NAME SHALL BE IN THEIR FOREHEADS.

AND THERE SHALL BE NO NIGHT THERE; AND THEY NEED NO CANDLE, NEITHER LIGHT OF THE SUN; FOR THE LORD GOD GIVETH THEM LIGHT: AND THEY SHALL REIGN FOR EVER AND EVER.

YOUR ORIGINAL ART

Matthew 5:1-12

King James Bible

And seeing the multitudes, He went up on a mountain, and when He was seated His disciples came to Him. Then He opened His mouth and taught them, saying:

"Blessed are the poor in spirit,
For theirs is the kingdom of heaven.
Blessed are those who mourn,
For they shall be comforted.
Blessed are the meek,
For they shall inherit the earth.
Blessed are those who hunger and thirst for righteousness,
For they shall be filled.
Blessed are the merciful,
For they shall obtain mercy.
Blessed are the pure in heart,
For they shall see God.
Blessed are the peacemakers,
For they shall be called sons of God.
10 Blessed are those who are persecuted for righteousness' sake,
For theirs is the kingdom of heaven.
Blessed are you when they revile and persecute you, and say all kinds of evil against you falsely for My sake. Rejoice and be exceedingly glad, for great is your reward in heaven, for so they persecuted the prophets who were before you."